阿
四

Also by Ting-xing Ye

A Leaf in the Bitter Wind

TING-XING YE

MY NAME IS NUMBER 4

A TRUE STORY FROM
THE CULTURAL REVOLUTION

THOMAS DUNNE BOOKS

ST. MARTIN'S GRIFFIN 🐾 NEW YORK

THOMAS DUNNE BOOKS.
An imprint of St. Martin's Press.

www.thomasdunnebooks.com
www.stmartins.com

Maps by William Bell

Library of Congress Cataloging-in-Publication Data

Ye, Ting-xing, 1952–
    My name is number 4 : a true story from the cultural revolution / Ting-xing Ye.—1st U.S. ed.
        p. cm.
    Abridged ed. of: A leaf in the bitter wind.
    Includes bibliographical references and index.
    ISBN-13: 978-0-312-37987-2 (alk. paper)
    ISBN-10: 0-312-37987-0 (alk. paper)
    1. Ye, Ting-xing, 1952– 2. China—Social conditions—1976–2000.
3. China—Social conditions—1949–1976. 4. Women—China—Biography.
I. Title. II. Title: My name is number four.

HN733.5.Y42 2008
365'.45092—dc22
[B]

2008021503

Abridged edition of: *A Leaf in the Bitter Wind*

First published in Canada by Doubleday Canada, a division of
Random House of Canada Limited

First U.S. Edition: September 2008

10 9 8 7 6 5 4 3 2 1

for my brothers

Ye Zheng-xing
Ye Zhong-xing

and my sisters

Ye Shen-xing
Ye Feng-xing

A NOTE ON CHINESE PRONUNCIATION

I have used the *han yu pin yin* system of romanization. A few names such as Yangtze and Chiang Kai-shek have been left in the older spelling because *pin yin* forms might be unfamiliar. English-speaking readers will find that most letters in *pin yin* are pronounced more or less the same as those in English. Some exceptions are:

c = ts, as in pe*ts*
q = ch, as in chur*ch*
x = *hss*
z = dz, as in a*dze*
zh = j, as in juice

AUTHOR'S NOTE

The words *Lao* (Old, Venerable) and *Xiao* (Young) when used with a surname are common terms of respect in China. Thus, I was usually addressed as Xiao Ye by persons outside my family.

With the exception of public figures and members of my family, I have disguised the names of all Chinese persons in this book.

ACKNOWLEDGEMENTS

I want to thank my publisher, Maya Mavjee, for supporting this project; my editor, Amy Black, for believing in this book and for helpful suggestions and encouragement; William Bell, as always, for everything.

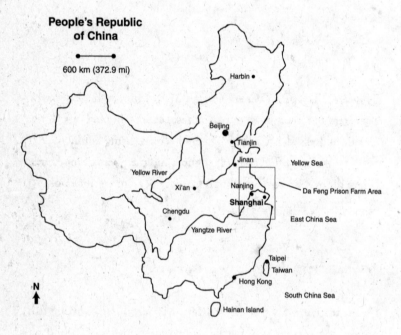

DA FENG PRISON FARM AREA

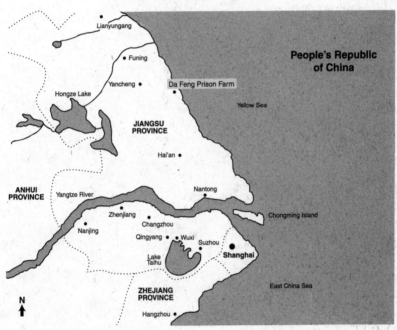

PART ONE

—

INTO THE BITTER SEA

PROLOGUE

—

The morning of my exile to the prison farm arrived, a characteristic November day in Shanghai, damp and chilly with an overcast sky. My two older brothers silently wrapped my wooden boxes and bedroll with thick straw ropes against the long rough journey. For lunch Great-Aunt made my favourite meal: pork chops Shanghai-style, with green onions. I ate hardly a mouthful, nor did my brothers and sisters. After the dishes were cleaned up, Great-Aunt told us she was going to her regular newspaper-reading meeting and, without saying goodbye or wishing me a safe journey, without looking at me, she left and closed the door behind her.

An hour later, I left my home, wondering if I would ever again walk in those three rooms, sleep in Great-Aunt's bed or stand in the sky-well and look up at the room where my parents had lived and died. My sisters and brothers and I trudged down Purple Sunshine Lane, where I had played and chased sparrows, where I had walked white-clad in two funeral processions. We passed my old temple school and the market where I had lined up many times to buy rice and pork bones. On the way to the bus stop we had to pass the building where Great-Aunt had her meeting. I saw her sitting in the doorway, weeping. I stopped and tried to speak. I wanted to tell her how much I loved her, but she looked away.

When we arrived at the district sports centre, where all the exiles had been ordered to assemble, my brothers set down my luggage. They and my two sisters stood awkwardly, at a loss for words. My younger sister, Number 5, was crying; Number 3 stared at the damp sidewalk. The guards told me that only those going to the farm could enter the building. My final moment with my family had come. I let out a loud cry.

"Why can't they stay with me until I have to leave?" I begged.

It was no use.

At that moment someone shouted my name and through my tears I saw Teacher Chen running toward me. She had come to see me off. She assured my brothers and sisters that she would stay with me. I said a solemn goodbye to each of them, picked up my luggage and walked to the stadium door.

Teacher Chen persuaded the guard to let her accompany me inside, saying she represented the school. There were more than three hundred unhappy teenagers gathered inside, with bundles tightly packed and tied. Four other students from my school were also being sent away, Teacher Chen told me, but I didn't know them.

We sat down to wait. My teacher gave me some bread she had brought for me, but it stayed untouched. "Be proud of yourself, Xiao Ye," she said, trying to cheer me up. "You may only be 16, but you are not a coward."

I didn't feel brave at all.

It was getting dark when the loudspeakers called us to the waiting buses. As I was about to board, Teacher Chen held my hands in hers, in front of her chest. "Xiao Ye," she whispered, "remember the old saying, 'When at home, depend on your parents; when away from home, rely on your friends.' Make friends on the farm. They will help you."

I knew that in repeating this familiar old saying she was taking a risk, because most of the old proverbs had been denounced and she might be overheard. Everything is against me, I thought, even this proverb. I had no parents at home, and the Cultural Revolution, which encouraged friends to inform on one another, had destroyed friendship. There seemed nothing left to depend on, not even my shadow.

When I got on my bus, the fifth in line, there were no seats left. After stowing my luggage in the overhead racks, I stood in the aisle, wiping my eyes with my sleeve, as others were doing, and stared out the window. The bus passed through the gate into a street thronged with families and relatives who had been waiting for hours. Horns from passing vehicles honked. Bicycle bells rang out. People ran alongside the buses, shouting names and crying. When the buses came to a halt, dozens of hands were thrust into the windows, clutching the hands of loved ones. I searched the crowd for my sisters and brothers.

The bus lurched and began to move forward again. The hands at the windows gradually fell away. Then I heard desperate shouting. "Ah Si! Ah Si! Where are you?"

I pushed and squeezed my way to a window, ignoring the protests of those in the seats.

"Here! Here!" I yelled.

Then I saw Number 1 checking the buses ahead of me, waving and calling out my name as each one passed him.

"Number 1, I'm here!" I cried out.

The bus sped up. My brother ran alongside, stretching his hand to the window. More than anything I wanted that one last touch. I reached out the window as far as I could, opening and closing my hand, but Number 1 fell back and I felt only cold air.

CHAPTER ONE

—

I was born in Shanghai, late on a hot June afternoon in 1952, the fourth child in my family. So I was called Ah Si, Number 4.

My father decided four kids were enough, but rather than rely on birth control, which was officially discouraged at that time, he put his faith in the power of words. Choosing a formal name for a child was no small matter: it required the weighing of tradition and precedent.

My surname, Ye, means Leaf. My generation name, Xing—Capable—had been decreed by my paternal grandfather after casting bamboo fortune telling sticks in the family ancestral hall, so all Father's children were called Xing. My three older siblings Father had named after characteristics he admired; my brothers were Upright and

Steadfast, my sister Diligent. For me he chose Ting, a homonym that means Graceful in writing but sounds like Stop when heard.

The word magic didn't work. A year and a half later my sister Maple was born, Mother's fifth and last child.

Normally, June was the beginning of the rainy season, a time of year hated by most people in the lower reaches of the Yangtze River. There was usually a solid month of drizzle and extreme humidity. Green mould grew on walls and floors; dampness seeped into people's bones. On the rare days when the sun appeared, courtyards and sidewalks were festooned with clothing, bedding and furniture. Everyone dreamt of living in a "zipper-roofed building."

As Great-Aunt never tired of telling anyone who would listen, my coming into the world was unlucky, a girl born in the year of the dragon.[1] She also said I was destined to lead a hard and unpredictable life, since June 1952 was uncharacteristically hot and dry, a sure sign of the King Dragon's disapproval, for he was the God of Rain. King Dragon, she said, dwelt in a crystal palace at the bottom of the Eastern Sea, where he was surrounded by crab generals and an army of shrimps, all of them male. I was often tempted to ask who did the household chores if there were no females like Grandmother, Mother

---

[1] Although we called her Great-Aunt, she was not a blood relation. She had been taken into my grandfather Ye's household as an unpaid live-in maid when in her twenties, after being twice widowed. When my father set up his home in Shanghai, Great-Aunt was sent along to keep house for him.

(Left) My paternal grandfather, Ye You-quan, who was severely beaten by Red Guards because he once owned land and a business.
(Right) My great-aunt, Chen Feng-mei, given to my family as a housemaid by her mother after two arranged marriages didn't work out.

and Great-Aunt herself around. But I had learned at an early age that there were two topics I should never question: the gods and the government.

———

A week after my birth, Mother brought me home from the Red House Hospital, so named because red paint covered its brick walls, wooden window-frames and doors, to my family's three-room apartment in the centre of the city. Shaded by plane trees, Wuding (Valiant Tranquillity) Road ran east and west through the former International Settlement and many

The main street of the town of Qingyang, where my father was born and raised.

long-tang—lanes, some as wide as two cars side by side, some only shoulder width—connected with it, forming a densely populated yet quiet neighbourhood. Shanghai itself, only ten miles wide and ten miles long, was inhabited by about six million people. We lived in Zi Yang Li—Purple Sunshine Lane.

Our two-story brick building was a traditional Shanghai-style house, built in a square U-shape around a courtyard or "sky-well" that served as the front entrance. Two black-lacquer doors, heavy and tall, with brass door-knockers shaped like dragon heads with rings through their noses, guarded the courtyard. Residents used the back door, however, reserving the front for occasions such as weddings and funerals.

In all, eight families lived in six apartments, three at each level. Two water taps in the tiny corridor at the back served all the families, and their use was strictly regulated and policed by our neighbour, Granny Ningbo. The upper tap, with its brick sink, could be used only to wash food, clothing and dishes. The lower one was for cleaning chamber pots and rinsing mops. On each floor, one small kitchen served four families. From the roof terrace I could see the chimney of the Zheng Tai Rubber Shoe Factory, which my father owned.

Where Purple Sunshine Lane intersected with Wuding Road was the *cai chang*—food market. Its rough plank stalls

(Left) The "stone arched" house in Purple Sunshine Lane, downtown Shanghai, where I was born and raised.
(Right) My four siblings and I in 1956. Back row, left to right: second eldest brother, Number 2; eldest brother, Number 1. Front row, left to right: me; younger sister, Number 5; elder sister, Number 3.

(Left) Number 3 and I, autumn 1957.
(Right) Purple Sunshine Lane, showing laundry drying on bamboo
poles overhead.

stretched about thirty yards along both sides of the shady
street. The centre of our neighbourhood, it opened at six
o'clock in the morning, but lineups for popular food like pork
bones and fat, which were cheaper and required fewer ration
coupons, began to form hours earlier. Some residents would
get out of bed early, take up spots near the front of the line,
then sell them for a few cents. By early afternoon the market
was closed, and the residents used the empty stalls to make
quilts on or to air their bedding.

For several years the sky-well, the lane and the busy market
were my world.

———

One day when I was four years old, my father came home from the factory with a big red silk flower pinned to the lapel of his Western-style jacket. Even at that age I knew that wearing a red flower, real or not, meant praise and honour. But Father didn't look happy about his prize. He limped past me, tossing the flower on the dinner table, and closed the bedroom door behind him. I stared longingly at the red blossom. From inside the bedroom, I heard Father and Mother talking. Only then did I realize that Father had come home early. All my older siblings were still in school and two-year-old Number 5 was having a nap.

Mother came out of the room and saw me eyeing the flower. She said I could have it so long as I kept quiet. She helped me pin it to my jacket and I rushed joyfully downstairs to the sky-well, sporting my colourful reward. I didn't know that Father had been given the flower for surrendering his factory—the enterprise his grandfather had established and he had operated for almost twenty years—to the government. In return, he was to receive a ridiculously meagre compensation of cash and bonds, paid in installments over seven years.[2]

Father was kept on as "private representative" to run the factory he used to own. But when he insisted on claiming his compensation, he was labelled a "hard-minded capitalist" who, the government said, could be reformed only through hard physical labour. Thus, before I turned five, my father

---

[2] In 1956 the government began its nationalization program: the forced confiscation of all private businesses.

had fallen from a respected and prosperous business owner to a labourer.

Even though I was too young to understand the momentous changes that worried Mother, Father and Great-Aunt, I was old enough to notice certain changes. Father no longer wore his Western-style jacket and tie. Instead he put on a dark blue or black worker's jacket buttoned up to the neck. Despite his physical disability—a childhood attack of meningitis had crippled him in one leg and he had to walk with a cane—he was assigned to one of the most menial jobs in the factory, pushing a heavy wooden cart loaded with rubber shoe uppers between workshops. It was the humiliation and deep wound to his pride that led him to make a decision that turned to tragedy.

One morning in April 1959, Father left home to go to work as usual. It was the last time I saw him walk. Later that day, Mother was called to a district hospital, where she learned that without telling anyone in the family Father had undergone surgery to cure his limp. The operation had been botched and Father was paralyzed from the waist down. Mother was horrified to see Father's entire torso wrapped in bandages that hid a wide scar from the base of his neck to his pelvis. After three years of suffering, confined to his bed, he passed away at the age of forty-one. I was nine.

Left with five kids and no job, my mother took me time after time on her visits to the factory, where she begged the officials to cash some of the bonds Father had been given when the factory was expropriated. The family had no income now, she argued, and her children were hungry. Her pleas and my tears had no effect. The bonds could not be redeemed for many years, Mother was reminded.

In order to feed her family, Mother had to face the fact that one of my brothers, seventeen and fifteen at the time, would have to quit school and find a job. One day in May 1963, a year after Father's death, Mother once again took me with her to the factory. She asked the director to take one of her sons on as an apprentice to help ease her burden and support the family. If there was any way she could have avoided coming to him for help, she said, weeping harder, she wouldn't be sitting there begging him. An hour later, we were sent away without an answer.

For weeks the atmosphere at home was so tense that I could almost touch it with my fingertips: tense because my brothers were forced to make a decision neither of them wanted; tense because the factory director might turn down Mother's pleas. Finally the answer came: the Rubber Industry Department would take Number 1 on, not in Father's factory, but in one that specialized in melting and refining raw rubber.

Mother was relieved but worried. She had wanted her son to work in Father's former factory because it was nearby. Most of the workers there knew our family and she hoped that they would look after her son. An added complication was that, although the director had specified a position for my eldest brother, Number 1 and Number 2 had decided differently. None of us knew how they had come to the conclusion that Number 2 was to be the one to quit school so that Number 1, who was one year short of qualifying to sit for university exams, could continue his education. My father had always wanted both of his sons to go to university. Since no one in the new factory knew my family, Number 2 pretended to be Number 1, and by the time the director found out, Number 2 had turned sixteen and was already a skillful worker.

So by the time I was twelve, my family had been on welfare for years. Where I had once sported a silk coat covered with a cotton smock, I now wore my brother's hand-me-downs. And when I passed up and down our lane, the residents, in particular the members of the neighbourhood committee,[3] suspicious that my "capitalist" mother had secret income, would stop me and lift up my jacket to make sure I wasn't wearing good clothing hidden underneath. When I became nearsighted, Mother ignored my pleas for prescription glasses because she couldn't afford to buy me a pair. Instead she gave me a pair Number 2 had outgrown. They caused me constant headaches, and I put them on only when necessary.

However, my personality had grown far from the modest and passive Chinese female praised by tradition. In defending myself and my family's name and, at times, fighting

---

[3.] The neighbourhood committee is the lowest level of government organization. It puts government regulations into effect at "street level," for example, distribution of food and coal coupons, or administration of welfare payments.

against my bullying neighbours over my mother, I became combative and argumentative. This often saddened Mother. The degradation of poverty and social discrimination had left deep scars.

Our household, meanwhile, struggled to return to normal. In August 1964, I was accepted by an all-girl middle school named Ai Guo—Love Your Country—which had been run by foreign missionaries before the communist government came to power.[4] My sister, Number 3, was enrolled in a new middle school closer to home. Number 1, after scoring extremely high on his entrance exams, won a place at the coveted Jiao Tong University in Shanghai. In five years, he would be an automotive engineer. Mother was especially happy to see Number 2 spending more time at Father's desk. He had been admitted to a workers' night school and was taking courses to complete his senior middle school education.

But throughout the fall of 1964, Mother continuously lost weight. She insisted that everything was fine but I frequently saw her holding a hot-water bottle to her stomach. Then one day, her pain drove her to the hospital. The diagnosis was final and devastating: cancer. Two-thirds of Mother's stomach was removed. We should hope for the best, the doctor said to the five of us.

Six months later, the cancer returned. This time Mother was sent home from the hospital with a gloomy prognosis and

---

[4] In China, middle school is divided into junior (grades 7–9) and senior (grades 10–12).

a large dose of painkillers. On December 31, 1965, after enduring months of awful pain and misery, Mother too died, three years after Father had left us.

In the days after Mother's funeral, I refused to go to school. In fact, I felt I wouldn't mind if I never saw my classroom again. The sight of my parents' silent bedroom and empty bed frightened me. I was scared to stay home yet scared to go out.

The spring passed slowly as the five of us tried to face our parentless life. In March, Great-Aunt turned 55 and was retired from the factory. She was home all day. Yet her care and devotion to us made me miss my mother more than ever.

(Left) My mother, Li Xiu-feng, Shanghai, 1948, just before Mao Ze-dong proclaimed the founding of the People's Republic of China.
(Right) My father, Ye Rong-ting, Shanghai, 1948.

—

One warm April morning, two months before my fourteenth birthday, I was busily working at my desk during a break between classes. Most of us at Ai Guo Middle School used the recess time to make a start on our homework so we would have less to do after school. As I got out of my seat to head for the bathroom I felt something warm and sticky running down the inside of my leg. One of the girls sitting behind me cried out, pointing to the floor, "Look! Blood!" The other girls craned their necks and whispered. There were red spots on the floor and a pool of blood on my seat.

Remembering Great-Aunt's gruesome tale of her cousin bleeding to death from a gastric ulcer, I was suddenly sick with terror. I have to get home, I thought frantically, snatching up my belongings and stuffing them into my bag. I adjusted the strap so the bag would cover my bottom and raced out of the school.

I ran all the way. First Father, then Mother. Now it was my turn to die, bleeding to death! I burst into our apartment and found Great-Aunt darning Number 2's cotton socks. She looked up, startled, as I squeezed past her, ducked behind the curtain and plunked myself down on the chamber pot.

"Great-Aunt," I cried, "I am bleeding to death, just like your cousin!"

"What are you talking about, Ah Si?" Through a gap in the curtain I noted that she hadn't even looked up from her mending.

"I have blood all over my pants and it's still coming!" I yelled. What's wrong with her? I thought. Can't she see I'm sick?

19

Finally she put down the sock and needle and slowly rose to her feet, mumbling.

"What did you say?" I shouted, exasperated by her apparent calm.

"I really don't know what to tell you," she said, opening a dresser drawer. "It should be a mother's job to explain this."

I hated it when she talked like that. Whenever I got on her nerves, she wouldn't criticize me. Instead, she would blame Mother for spoiling me. If I complained about the ugliness of my clothes, she would say I had Mother's vanity in my blood. I had given up arguing years ago; she always got the last word.

Now here we go again, I thought. I'm dying and she makes remarks about my poor dead mother.

"Why can't you leave Mother alone? At least you're still alive."

I yanked the curtain closed, expecting her to criticize me for my outburst. But she brought me a small paper parcel and a square brown package with "Sanitary Paper" written on all four sides. Her lack of concern calmed me somewhat and I examined the parcel. I had seen ones like it in store windows and had often wondered why there were two kinds of toilet paper, one called straw paper—an accurate description, since smashed straw pieces made a wrongful appearance here and there—and the other sanitary paper, which was sold in glued packages rather than stacks. Now that I thought of it, I had also seen it from time to time in our toilet paper basket at home.

But why was Great-Aunt handing me this stuff when I was in such danger? My very life was flowing down my legs.

I recalled what the doctor had told us when he had diagnosed Mother's terminal cancer: "Let her eat what she likes." Was that why Great-Aunt was giving me such fancy toilet paper?

I turned the second packet over in my hand. "Sanitary Belt," it read. I thought, double sanitation. Inside was a pink belt-like contraption, shaped like the letter T, made of soft rubber with white cotton bands.

"What's this?" I called out to Great-Aunt, who had returned to her work. "Why are you giving me these instead of pills?"

"Are you really as stupid as you sound? Can't you read?"

"Of course I can, but there's nothing here to tell me what they're for!"

"Don't try to fool me. I may not know how to read, but I can see there are words all over the packages," she insisted.

Knowing I had already gone too far, I softened a bit. Besides, I knew I could be left in this position all day if I opened my mouth again. In a moment Great-Aunt came back and showed me how to fit the paper inside the belt.

"Believe me, you are not going to die. Your parents wouldn't let that happen to you."

I put the strange contraption on and waited for Number 3 to come home for lunch. She went to a different school because of her entrance exam results. Maybe I could get some answers as well as sympathy from my elder sister.

"Number 3! I thought I was going to die this mor—"

"Cut your voice down, Ah Si," Great-Aunt interrupted.

"What happened?" Number 3 asked.

I dragged her into the front room. "I have gastric bleeding, just like Great-Aunt's cousin. You can't imagine what a mess I made in the classroom."

Before I could go on, my sister pushed me away. "It's a pity you only look smart," she sneered. "Didn't you read your health textbook?" She walked out of the room, muttering, "Dying! As if there isn't enough death in this family already."

Physiological Hygiene was a non-credit course at my school. We had one lecture a week and were supposed to study the textbook ourselves. But the lectures were often cancelled to make time for political study sessions, and I had avoided the book ever since a girl in my class had been accused of having dirty thoughts when she was spotted looking at the pictures of a naked man and woman.

That afternoon I hunted up the book. By the time I had finished reading it, I was weeping, for the relevant section emphasized that students should read it "under parental guidance."

I felt Great-Aunt's hand on my shoulder. "Don't be sad, Ah Si. Every girl has to go through this, and believe it or not, some parents are happy for their daughters when it happens."

"The book says it's a mother's job to tell things like this to their daughters," I said without looking at her. "But Mother is gone. Who is going to tell me all the rest of the things I don't know?"

"Ah Si, I'll try, if you let me. I'll do my best to raise you, even though I'm not sure how."

I now felt sorry for the words I had thrown at her earlier.

Probably nobody had ever told Great-Aunt herself about menstruation. And I was sure there had been no book available for her, even if she had been able to read. Considering her own life, how could she say that for a young girl to become a woman was a joy?

The harmony we had reached was short-lived, though. Before supper time I asked her for another package of sanitary paper.

"Are you saying you used it all in less than half a day?" She sounded more shocked than angry.

"Well, I didn't eat it! It's paper, you know, not candy."

"Each package costs thirty cents," she rebuked me as she showed me how to extend the life of the paper by refolding it for a second use. "That was half a day's pay for your brother when he was an apprentice."

How nice it would be if there was just one thing in life that didn't involve money. Only a few days before, she had been complaining loudly about the rise in food prices. How could she save money for our winter clothes? I pictured our money flying away with all the sanitary paper for Number 3, Great-Aunt and me. One day Number 5 would need it too.

I sighed. "Great-Aunt, wouldn't it be wonderful if we were all boys?"

———

One dusty and windy afternoon toward the end of May, fifty classmates and I rode the bus for an hour and a half into

Songjiang County to the Eastern Town Brigade. Although my visits to Grandfather's rural town had made me familiar with country living, I was nervous and confused. We had been sent there to help with the Three Summer Jobs, a policy that had more to do with politics than logic, and I had no idea how we city girls could help the peasants. In the space of two weeks we were supposed to learn planting, harvesting and field manage-ment, and to grow physically and mentally fit from hard labour. We were housed in a large building with a swept dirt floor. Along the walls, rice straw had been strewn over planks for our beds. I dropped my bedroll onto the boards and started to unpack.

It turned out that there was not as much "real work" as we had been led to expect. First, we picked up loose ears of wheat in the fields and along the roads, an easy but tremen-dously tedious job. A few days later, we carried bundles of rapeseed stalks, which had been harvested and tied loosely with straw. Since the seed pods were crisp and fell off easily, great care was needed when transporting them to the thresh-ing ground. The farmers instructed us to carry one bundle at a time, but we all burst out laughing after lifting them up: the large, awkward bundles seemed weightless. Ignoring the expert advice, we left with one bundle in each hand, strug-gling over the ridges in the plowed fields. A strong wind buffeted the bundles like kites, pulling me this way and that until I lost balance and fell to the dirt. Rapeseed scattered and rolled all around me. By the end of the day at least five of us had sprained our ankles.

Some villagers didn't hide their feelings about the whole business of having incompetent city kids around, calling our mission "lighting a candle for a blind person," and all of us eagerly awaited the day when we could go home. When we stepped down from the bus into our schoolyard two weeks later I felt we had not gained much except our bundles of dirty laundry. Principal Lin welcomed us back with a long boring speech, during which he constantly consulted his notebook as we stood baking in the sun.

"The physical achievement of your hard work is not nearly as important as your mental accomplishment through living with the peasants, the best teachers in life," he began.

As he droned on, he kept glancing nervously at the school's Communist Party Secretary Fang, who stood to the side in the shadows. Something is up, I thought. Principal Lin went on to say that, contrary to custom, we would not have the next day off to rest. We must return to school. That was when Secretary Fang cut in.[5]

He announced that all our regular classes would be suspended until further notice. We had a lot of catching up to do in our political education, he said. We would be studying documents from the Central Committee of the Communist Party—the "May 7th Directive," the "16th Circular" and editorials from

---

[5.] Every organization or work unit (called a *dan wei*) in China—school, factory, the government itself—had an administrative head and a Party Secretary. All policies and decisions required the Secretary's approval. He or she was responsible for applying the Party's programs.

the *People's Daily* newspaper, the main mouthpiece of the Party. Drooping in the heat, I paid little attention when he declared that a new movement was about to start.

When I finally got home, Number 3 told me that her classes had been suspended as well. Number 5, who had been cramming and beavering through exercises in preparation for her middle-school entrance exams, had been thrown into endless meetings and discussions, too. She was delighted. After watching her four siblings killing themselves with study on previous occasions, she wanted none of it.

"I feel great!" she crowed. "No more burning the midnight oil, no more nightmares. I'm liberated!"

Number 3 didn't look so relieved. She had been sent home to write a *biao tai*—a statement of belief, repeating the government's policies—to make her position known in the new movement. I watched over her shoulder as she crossed out and revised her statement.

"I'd love to help, Ah Sei, but I have no idea what to suggest." I guess I didn't sound too sympathetic.

"Wait till it's your turn," she retorted.

Great-Aunt, too, was parroting new political terms, such as "a revolution that touches everyone's innermost being and purifies people's thinking." I laughed at her, for she clearly did not understand what she was saying.

We did not know it, but the Great Proletarian Cultural Revolution had begun.

CHAPTER TWO

—

"Suspend classes to make revolution!" was the first *da-zi-bao*—big character poster—I saw as soon as I walked through the front gate of my school the next morning.[6] I had left my school bag and lunch at home because there would be no classes and the steam room where our rice was cooked for us would not be operating. A second poster read, "Long Live the Great Proletarian Cultural Revolution!" Each black character on the blood-red paper was as tall as me.

Day after boring day our teachers read aloud to us government documents and newspaper editorials, which local and national papers were churning out with tedious regularity. This was the Party's method of spreading information about

---

[6.] A "character" in Chinese writing is equal to a word in English.

new policies and condemning or praising political figures, most of whom I had never heard of. Sometimes the teacher had us stand and read one paragraph each—a good method of keeping us awake. Soon we all sounded like Great-Aunt, spouting slogans and terms we didn't understand.

Like the other girls, I just went through the motions. This was not the first "movement" we had been forced to participate in: a few days short of fourteen years old, I was already a veteran. China—and our personal lives—fell under the control of the Communist Party. There was only one political party anyway, and Chairman Mao was the leader and ruled with an iron fist. Government officials were not elected by the people. Policies were forced on us through "campaigns." We all assumed that this latest campaign was directed mainly at people working in the Arts—those who, in Great-Aunt's words, "drink ink and play with pens." We thought it would be over in a few months; instead, it was to rage for ten years.

One morning I heard the school's loudspeakers blasting long before I entered the gate. "Fellow comrades, wield your pens as swords and spears and aim your words like bullets against the reactionaries." A reactionary was anyone who opposed the Party and government. "Go to collect your weapons at the main office."

The office had been turned into a storehouse stacked with giant sheets of coloured paper, boxes of bottled ink and writing brushes of all sizes. In one corner, Old Uncle Zhang, the gatekeeper, was making glue in a wooden barrel to paste up the posters. His forehead shone with sweat and his shirt clung to his back. A chattering human stream flowed through the room, picking up supplies for the writing of *da-zi-bao* and *xiao-zi-bao*—the second being small character posters written with pen rather than brush.

I left with a bottle of ink, two brushes and a sheaf of red paper under my arm. At the foot of the stairs leading to my classroom, two freshly hung posters, the ink still running, caught my eye. "Rebellion is justified!" screamed the first. The second filled me with confusion and dread: "If Lin Guang-min does not surrender, we will destroy him!" The three characters of our principal's name had been crossed over with Xs. Years before I had seen many caricatures of John F. Kennedy—whose name was transcribed into Chinese as *ken-ni-di*—chew the dirt floor. On those posters, each character in Kennedy's name had been over-written with an X to show he was an enemy.

I stood transfixed. Principal Lin, in his late fifties, was well respected by the teachers and students, a man who would "check the ground before taking a step, for fear of crushing an ant," as my geography teacher put it. What had he done to justify such extreme disrespect?

Shaken and confused, I spent the rest of the day filling my large red sheet with pointless slogans. While I was gluing my poster up on a brick wall I noticed that some of those already hung accused Principal Lin of "using ancient things to make fun of the present" in his history classes. Most of them were signed by "Revolutionary Soldiers," even though pupils had written them.

The next day I found my previous day's labour plastered over with new and more aggressive posters. I had never seen the students in such high spirits: no classes, no school, no homework and, most of all, free to criticize teachers, an unprecedented event since the time of Confucius, who had emphasized that teachers should always be treated with honour and respect.

The colourful posters attacked teachers for giving low marks or for writing critical remarks on report cards, and some exposed their private lives through gossip and rumour. One related that a pretty young math teacher, Yao, had shared a boiled egg with a bachelor teacher, Meng. Yao ate only the yolk and Meng finished the rest. They were openly addressed as "Teacher Yolk" and "Teacher Egg-white" by the students. Another poster disclosed that the only son of Teacher Zhu, my first-year English instructor, was adopted. The cruelty and meanness of this gossip was enormous. Adopting someone in your extended family was not uncommon in China, but adoption from outside was widely considered "fetching water with a bamboo-woven basket"—a futile effort—owing to traditional attitudes toward blood lineage. As a result, adoptive parents never revealed the truth to the child and would often move to another neighbourhood, even change jobs if possible, to keep the secret.

Not content with this, the poster writer also accused Teacher Zhu of refusing to have her own child out of vanity, "concerned that bearing a child will destroy her figure"—a rotten bourgeois way of thinking. I saw my former teacher standing in front of the poster, vainly trying to explain to the girls surrounding her that the charge was untrue. She could not have children, she said. She would show them her medical records.

Unable to bear seeing her degradation, and sensing that no matter what she said, no one would listen to her, I stole away. All the way home I wished I could take back the unkind thoughts I had had about her when she gave me a low mark on my assignment. What will come next? I wondered. Whose turn will it be?

I arrived at school late the following day to find a circle of screaming girls surrounding Teacher Zhu near the auditorium. Pale and exhausted, she stood with her narrow shoulders hunched and her head down. The sight sickened and terrified me.

"What did you mean," someone shouted, "when you taught us that 'Long live Chairman Mao' means 'Chairman Mao lives long'?" It was one of my own classmates, Tang, nicknamed "Super Flat" because of the unusual flatness of her head and face. In two years I had never heard her utter a word in class. Now here she was attacking our teacher over a point of grammar. None of us had been able to understand how to translate "Long live Chairman Mao" because we had not yet studied the subjunctive mood, so Teacher Zhu had suggested that for the time being we take it as "Chairman Mao lives long."

"We all wish that Chairman Mao will live forever, but you said he just lives for a long time," my classmate shrieked. "How long did you have in mind? What was your real purpose? Confess!"

The girls immediately broke into a chant. "*Wan-shou-wu-jiang! Wan-shou-wu-jiang!*—May our great leader Chairman Mao live forever!" They waved a little book as they chased my teacher across the schoolyard.

I realized that almost everyone had a red book except me, and, frightened by the attack on Teacher Zhu, I figured I'd better get one quickly. I headed for the main office, where two students sat behind a desk piled high with plastic covered volumes with *Quotations of Chairman Mao* embossed on the red plastic cover. I gave them my name and grade.

"What is your class background?" the heaviest of the two demanded.

All the political turmoil that had swirled through my school, all the personal attacks on teachers, should have made me more careful, but I was still naive. I answered.

"*Zi-chan-jie-ji*—capitalist class."

"Then you don't deserve one," came the angry reply. "The red treasure books are for students who are from the Five Reds, not for your stinking shitty class, who exploit the workers!"

In the files kept by the police on everyone, the most important item of information was your social "class." People who were peasants or workers like Great-Aunt were good; landlords or business owners were bad. Because my grandfather Ye had once owned land and my father had owned a factory, my family was classified as capitalist, even though Father's business was gone.

I couldn't believe my ears. I looked around for a teacher to help or at least tell me what was going on, but none was in sight. What were the Five Reds? All I knew was that red meant good and black was bad. What could they mean calling me an exploiter and member of a shitty class? My family was poor and I was living on welfare. I felt the tears sting my eyes, but refused to let them out.

"You don't need to insult me," I said. "If you don't want to give me the book, I'll be fine without it." And I ran from the office and out of the school. When I got home I broke down. I had thought that I would never cry like that again, never after my parents died. Great-Aunt listened without interruption, then went to her dresser and returned with a red book in her hand.

"Ah Si, take mine," she offered. "When the neighbourhood committee gave it to me I didn't know what it was. All I can recognize is the portrait of Chairman Mao."

"You don't understand!" I shot back. "I'm not crying because I don't have this book. It's the insult. I don't deserve to be degraded like that. Calling me 'shit'!" I threw down her book and stormed out of the room.

As if I was not upset enough, Number 3 came home with a copy of the red book. When I retold my tale of woe, she burst out laughing, saying I was "brainless" and lacked "flexible thinking."

"Why did you tell them the truth?" she sneered. "Did you think they would bother to check? These books come by the truckload! I told them I am a daughter of an office clerk, not totally untrue. Father did work in an office and did clerical and accounting work, didn't he? It all depends on your point of view. Smarten up, Ah Si!"

I must have looked astonished. Was this what she meant when she said I was not "flexible"?

That night, Number 2 explained to me who the Five Reds were: factory workers, poor and lower-middle-class peasants, soldiers and officers of the People's Liberation Army, Party officials, and revolutionary martyrs. The families of these five categories were therefore "red" also. In contrast, the Five Blacks included former landlords, rich peasants, counter-revolutionaries, rightists, and former capitalists.

I was furious that my family was included in the Five Blacks, but puzzled as well. How could we be capitalists? We had been born and had grown up under the Communist flag. Our so-called capitalist parents were dead. We were poor. We didn't own anything.

I made up my mind before I went to bed that I was not going back to school the next day no matter what Great-Aunt said. To my surprise, she didn't object, and I passed my time at home, reading and snoozing. Each afternoon Number 3 told me what was going on in her school. More teachers were publicly denounced and locked up in sheds. Students belonging to the Five Reds were calling for "revolution around the clock" and had turned the classrooms into dorms, refusing to go home. A "work team" composed of factory workers and government officials had been stationed in her school and was encouraging the students to "blast the lid off the class struggle."

"I don't know how long you can stay home like this, Ah Si," Number 3 warned. "They have a name for people like you now—idlers—and you won't be able to get away with it for long."

CHAPTER THREE

—

About two weeks later, at the beginning of August, Number 5 burst through the door in tears.

"My classmates called me dirty names and told me that our father was an exploiter!" she wept. "Ah Si, I can't even remember what Father looked like. I was so young when he died. I didn't even know what he did for a living. How come the others know all that?"

She had cried all the way home because she had been rejected by the *Hong Xiao Bing*—Little Red Guards—because of her family background. I was unable to comfort her.

Recently, Mao had called upon young people, those still in school or university, to carry on the struggle to make revolution. He named them Red Guards. But to be a Red Guard you had to be from a politically "pure"—red—family.

I myself was worried about the summons signed by Red Guards ordering me to report to them at my school. Great-Aunt had often said that if you have done nothing wrong you needn't be frightened by a pounding on your door in the middle of the night. The next morning, I repeated the saying to myself as I walked along. If attacked for being an idler, I planned to confess my "lack of revolutionary spirit," hoping that would satisfy them enough to leave me alone.

The street outside the school was ablaze with big character posters. "Smash So-and-so's dog head!" "Flog the cur that has fallen into the water!" (Be merciless with bad people even if they are down.) One poster declared the establishment of the school's Red Guards, ending with, "It is right to rebel against reactionaries!"

When I arrived at the school gate house, Old Uncle Zhang was not there as he usually was. I recognized all of the occupants there in his place except two young women dressed in faded army fatigues with red armbands. *Hong Wei Bing*—Red Guards—was written in yellow.

I was challenged by a knot of girls at the gate. "State your class background," one of them shouted. There was no time to use the ruse Number 3 had suggested, for one of the girls recognized me and pointed her finger. "She's the one who told me she could get along just fine without the treasure book!"

One of the strangers strutted over and stood in front of me. She was much taller than me and solidly built.

"You son-of-a-bitch capitalist!" she hissed. Her accent told me she was a Northerner. I hung my head, hoping not too many of my schoolmates had heard the insulting remark. She punched my shoulder to straighten me up. "Go to the side door. We will deal with you later."

Frightened, I did as I was told. As soon as I entered the side gate I was confronted by three Red Guards. My name and class background were taken down and I was directed to a Red Guard whose armband indicated that she was from Dong Chen District, Beijing, the capital city. She stood, sweating in her ill-fitting army uniform, cap pulled down tightly, armpits mapped with perspiration, thumbs in her belt in a pose praised by Mao, who had written that Chinese women preferred battle fatigues to silk. She ordered me to join six other students who stood facing a brick wall. I knew all of them. They were always well dressed and a few were members of the students' council, a prestigious position in most people's eyes, including mine. Not one of them said a word to me. I got the feeling that it was not their first experience staring at the wall, so I followed their lead, and stood still, looking down at my cotton shoes.

Although it was not yet nine o'clock, the heat was stifling, beating down on us and radiating from the wall. By noon—I could tell the hour by the slow progress of our shadows—there were about two dozen of us wilting in line. Finally the Beijing Red Guard led us away toward the schoolyard. There weren't many students there; most had been driven indoors by the sweltering heat. The dirt yard was like a laundry with crisp, faded paper sheets hung from numerous clotheslines strung from side to side.

"You are ordered to read all the *da-zi-bao* and then report to me before you go home," she shouted. "Maybe we can drive some stinking capitalist ideas from your heads."

Walking between the rows of hanging posters, I not only found many duplicates and copied newspaper articles, I noticed that some of the writers had inadvertently omitted half sentences or entire paragraphs, making the poster meaningless. They were all signed "East Is Red" or "Defending the East" or "Revolutionary Masses" or "Red Rebels." How ridiculous, I thought.

But I felt a chill when I saw that Teacher Zhang, my second-year English instructor, had been denounced. Someone had listed the names of her and her five siblings, circling the middle character of each name. The linked characters read "Long Live the Republic of China."

I knew Teacher Zhang was in big trouble. The Republic of China, not the People's Republic of China, was how the previous government referred to my country before the Communists took over. To show the slightest loyalty to the old rulers was treason. But why blame Teacher Zhang? Why not blame her father? It was he who named his children.

Number 1 was at home a lot, since the university too was in turmoil and all classes were suspended in favour of endless political study. That night I asked him about Teacher Zhang's case. He said that obviously all the children in her family had been born when the Nationalists were still in power and her father had found a smart way to show his loyalty to the regime. It was difficult to get a legal name change, he explained; there were as many procedures as hairs on an ox.

When I told him about the Beijing Red Guards, he grew agitated.

"Listen, Ah Si, do whatever you're told and never, ever argue or talk back. I know you too well. Your sharp tongue will get you in trouble. The Beijing Red Guards are the children of high Party officials. They have received Chairman Mao's support and they can be very dangerous if they get angry at you."

"There are no imported Red Guards at my school," Number 3 said. "They are probably punishing you for staying away from school, Ah Si."

Great-Aunt had stayed out of the conversation. When she and I were in bed she began to talk, staring at the ceiling. "It's you again, Ah Si, bullied by the Red Guards. Why does bad luck always follow you around? If that isn't Fate, what is it?" She let out a heavy sigh. "Your mother should have agreed when I offered to adopt you when you were a baby. Then you would be the daughter of a working-class woman and you would be safe."

—

I kept telling myself I would not let the Red Guards scare me any more, but as I got closer to school the next day my throat was dry and my legs were weak. For the first time I was grateful that none of my classmates lived in my lane and that the school was so far away. No one in my neighbourhood would witness my humiliation.

That thought brought to my mind one of Mao's sayings that had until recently begun our school day: "Good things can turn to bad things and vice versa." I had always wondered why this inane statement was the object of reverence, but maybe it held some truth after all. Before I reached the school I decided what I would put in my thought-report to the Red Guards. I would tell them that I now understood the Chairman's saying and that I had learned from my own experience how correct he was.

But I never got the chance. My group had apparently been treated "too leniently," walking around and reading posters. One of the Beijing Red Guards spouted from her red book: "Revolution is not a dinner party, nor is it writing articles, drawing pictures or doing embroidery; revolution is a class struggle of life and death." She divided us into work groups and set us to our "life and death struggle"—cleaning toilets and sweeping out the classrooms.

I knew that this assignment was not an effort to help the custodian and Old Uncle Zhang, who had been locked in a shed along with the principal because the Red Guards claimed that he was a spy for his former employer, the Christian mission school. As far as I could see, all he did was match our faces to the photos on our student cards every day as we passed through the school gate. I couldn't imagine poor illiterate Old Uncle Zhang spying for anyone.

So the hot days of August crept by. I had thought I would never sweep dirt floors again after I left the old temple school

I used to attend in our lane when I was little, but now I considered sweeping the back alley, mopping wooden floors and stairs and cleaning out the washrooms to be easy. On bad days I was yelled at and forced to write self-criticisms, complying with the Red Guards' shrill demands without hesitation. More than once I wondered what Mother would think, seeing her fourteen-year-old girl treated like an old-hand criminal.

CHAPTER FOUR

—

So far the Red Guards had wreaked havoc mainly inside the schools and universities, where they frequently beat teachers, sometimes to death, but an incident in Beijing raised their status dramatically. On August 18, Chairman Mao, wearing an army uniform, made an appearance at the Gate of the Heavenly Peace. He was formally presented with a Red Guard armband by a young woman named Song Bin-bin. *Bin-bin*—Genteel—is a fairly common name for a girl. Mao asked her, *"Yao-wu-ma?*—Do you want violence?"* At that moment, said the newspaper reports, the young woman accepted Mao's suggestion and changed her name to Song Yao-wu—Song Wants Violence.

Hundreds of thousands of young people throughout the country rushed to change their names to respond to Mao's call. And from that day the Red Guard movement, blessed by the Chairman himself, spread into the streets, its targets no longer limited to teachers. Mao Ze-dong had unleashed a violent windstorm that would engulf me and my siblings because we had been born to a capitalist father and mother who were no longer around to be attacked.

"Long live Chairman Mao! Long live the red sun in our hearts!" screamed the weeping Red Guards in my school when the news about Mao's blessing was announced. Armed with Mao's personal permission for violence and chaos, they swept from the school to "smash the Four Olds." This vague category of new enemies comprised old culture, old customs, old habits and old ways of thinking.

A few nights later a deafening racket of gongs, drums and shrill voices drew my sisters and me out of our apartment into the streets. Wuding Road was a turmoil of milling crowds, bonfires, shouted slogans. Number 3 and I walked around uneasy but fascinated, with Number 5 between us.

We watched as the Guards renamed our street: *Wuding* (Violent Tranquillity) became *Yaowu* (Desire for Violence) to echo Mao's call. We felt the heat of bonfires fed by books, paintings, embroidery and other "bourgeois goods" confiscated by the Red Guards when they raided local homes. Women with "bourgeois" hairstyles had their tresses hacked off in the street; men with haircuts that "looked like Kennedy" suffered the same humiliation. People wearing trousers with narrow legs were held down while the Red Guards took scissors and slashed the pants open. Those who wore pointed-toed leather shoes had them torn off their feet and hurled into the fire. Such "rotten Western" styles, the Guards screamed, must be driven out of China.

—

A few days later I was stopped on my way home from school by two girls who were not of the Five Reds nor Five Blacks, but were "Grays," children of shopkeepers, office clerks and elementary and middle-school teachers. They belonged to a Red Guard sub-unit, as they were not pure enough for the real thing.

I was fortunate, the girls brusquely informed me. The Guards were going to allow me to join an overnight parade to show Shanghai's support for the Great Proletarian Cultural Revolution. "Allowed" meant that I'd better turn up and take the opportunity to "educate and reform" myself. I resented their arrogance, but was secretly glad of the opportunity because I was sick of being the object of scorn and abuse at school. Maybe if I took part in the demonstration they wouldn't call me a shitty capitalist any more.

But I was worried that I could not endure a night-long parade. My period had started the day before. What would I do if the Guards did not let me leave the parade to visit a washroom?

To make matters worse, the hot, humid August weather was producing powerful winds and thunder, declaring the arrival of a typhoon. But the word came down: even if it rained knives, the parade would go on. The demonstration would show "our true revolutionary spirit as well as our determination to carry on the Cultural Revolution to the end."

As evening came on under threatening skies, Great-Aunt helped me prepare. She filled my school bag with sanitary paper, adding two extra pairs of underpants in case I needed them. By the time I fought my way through the wind and driving rain to the school, my umbrella had been pulled inside out and I was drenched. I was assigned to the tail end of our parade along with my "brick inspector" sisters, a name we had given ourselves after spending so many hours under the scalding sun, staring at the wall.

We began the slow march along dark streets in pounding rain. It took half an hour to get to the main road, where the congestion of thousands of converging marchers forced us to halt. By now the rain had stopped but the wind had ripped our flimsy paper flags away and we were left holding naked bamboo sticks. Larger red flags rippled and snapped; the black ink characters on the red cotton banners dissolved into meaningless blotches.

Still sodden, we stood buffeted by the gale for more than an hour. I was becoming desperate for a washroom so I could change my sanitary pad. I finally got the attention of a Red Guard and received her permission to leave the parade and go home with a girl who lived nearby. You-mei—Young Plum Blossom—took me to her family's apartment, which had a huge carved steel door at the lane entrance. Her elderly parents were sitting in the living room, reading, oblivious to the political and atmospheric storms outside. You-mei showed me to a luxurious bathroom with a flush toilet, bathtub and sink. Embarrassed by the visit, I thanked them on my way out, turning my face away quickly so they would not recognize me if I met them again.

When we rejoined the still noisy parade it hadn't advanced an inch. The downpour began again. I wished I had a raincoat like most of the others, for it was hard to keep my bedraggled umbrella over my head in the wind. Time dragged. Still we remained rooted in the middle of the dark street. I began to think my daily sweating confinement at school was preferable to this cold and hungry vigil.

After midnight cramps gripped my abdomen again, but all the sanitary packages labouriously prepared by Great-Aunt were soaked. You-mei had disappeared and I could find no one else to take me to their home. Luckily it was dark and the stains on my soaking wet trousers would not show.

By now the crowd's enthusiasm had diminished. The flags had been rolled up and the banners put away. The chanting of slogans and shaking of fists and bamboo clubs had died down. Finally the word was passed down the stationary parade that our destination was People's Square downtown, where we would be reviewed by the mayor and other municipal officials. The news caused an enthusiastic stir, since being received by high officials was like being blessed by the Emperor in the old days.

But to me nothing would have been more exciting than finding a toilet. I began to understand the meaning of the word pilgrimage, which I had learned from reading the classic novel, *Journey to the West*. The night crept on; the rain beat down; the wind howled. My blood flow was heavy and I was growing weak. My teeth began to chatter and tremors shook my body.

At last, the parade began to move. We inched forward through the city streets until pale light showed in the sky.

As dawn arrived we entered People's Square. In the distance, so small I could hardly see them, three or four figures waved at us from a raised—and roofed—reviewing stand. No standing in the wind and rain for them. Moments later, the Red Guards ran up and down the ranks, telling us that the parade was over and we could go home.

The grateful crowd rapidly dispersed in all directions to bus and streetcar stops, but the transportation system had shut down for the parade. The hordes of marchers, like deflated rubber balls filling the streets, reminded me of the words Father had added to my composition six years before: "The crowd surged like a wave moving through water." Only now the water was a violent and bitter sea.

Exhausted by kilometres of marching and standing all through the rainy windy night, I began the three-kilometre walk home, chilled to the bone, drained by fatigue and loss of blood. When I woke up it was late afternoon and I found myself lying half on, half off Great-Aunt's bed in a pool of blood, my clothes still drenched with rain and blood from the night before. I dragged myself from the bed in a panic. It was no use: the blood had long since seeped through the straw mat and stained the bedding.

"Never mind, Ah Si," Great-Aunt waved off my apologies. "You have a hot bath and I'll take care of this."

Number 1 carried the water from downstairs and Number 3 brought me dry clothes. The hot bath was heavenly. After I had finished soaking, Great-Aunt prepared a cup of boiled ginger soup with brown sugar. I didn't tell her that I'd had to throw away the soaked and useless sanitary paper.

CHAPTER FIVE

—

When I returned to school in the first week of September, the Red Guards from Beijing had vanished. Nevertheless, the schoolyard looked uninviting, for the typhoon had swept almost all the posters to the ground, blocking the sewers with them, leaving puddles here and there dyed black with ink. This institution that should have been filled with happy schoolgirls at the beginning of a new school year had, in the past few months, been turned into a hateful vindictive place. And now it resembled a ghost town.

I turned and went home. Now, all of us except Number 2 had become idlers, and our lane was full of school kids just hanging around with nothing to do. I was glad to stay at home. But good things never last long. Late one afternoon when most families were preparing supper, we were once again drawn from our kitchens by the clamour of gongs and the racket of drums.

Some Beijing Red Guards led a group of a dozen local youths into our lane, marching slowly, beating their drums and gongs, shouting slogans against capitalists and counter-revolutionaries, checking the building numbers. Many of the onlookers—among them Boss Luo's wife from the building next to us, and my friend Ying-ying's mother—slunk away, no doubt hoping the raid would not be aimed at them.

To my relief, the noisy procession passed our door and stopped in front of Building Number 45. "Yao family! Show yourselves!" the leader shouted. Some Guards began to paste *da-zi-bao* on the laneway walls; others pushed into the Yaos' apartment, amid shouts of anger and terror.

The raids on our lane had been launched. In the days that followed, the neighbourhood was thronged with Red Guards. Old Yang, a worker at home with an injury, served as our information source, continuously updating his statistics. "So far, eighteen families have been searched. In Building 75 the Red Guards have taken the roof-drains apart to see if gold bars were hidden there. Now they are going through the roof tiles, looking for guns."

Our neighbours—and we—were terrified. Even a toy drum beating could halt a conversation. The raids spread to the houses near us, then right next door. I watched the attack through Great-Aunt's bedroom window as she sat on the bed mending socks. The Guards poured ink into dresser drawers and over chesterfields, enraged because they hadn't found the gold they thought would be there. They built a bonfire in the sky-well and burned books and paintings, old and new, hurling them into the flames from the upper windows. The senseless destruction horrified me. I wondered whether Great-Aunt still believed that if a person had done nothing wrong she had nothing to fear.

"Ah Si! Ah Si!" Number 1 shouted, bursting into the bedroom and slamming the windows shut before my eyes. "Come with me, now!"

My two sisters stood grim and silent in the front room. My parents' pride and joy had been our five antique Ming dynasty paintings, each more than two metres long and half a metre wide, done in traditional style. They were watercolours, mounted on silk, with rosewood scrolls at top and bottom. Four were landscapes depicting spring, summer, autumn and winter. The fifth, the centrepiece, portrayed three tigers so fierce and realistic they looked as though they might climb down from the wall and prowl the room. For my entire life they had hung on our walls. No one had ever thought about selling them to bring in much-needed cash.

Now the paintings were spread out on the floor. I looked questioningly at my brother. He was twenty years old now, the head of the family.

"These are the only things the Red Guards could punish us for," Number 1 said, his face bleak, his voice flat and determined.

We looked at each other.

"What would the Red Guards come here for? To look for gold?" I scoffed.

"If they do look for gold and jewels in the home of a welfare family it will show their stupidity," he responded, "but these paintings are antiques. They belong to the Four Olds. We have to show them a clean house because if they get angry at us there is no telling what might happen. People have been beaten to death for less."

Suddenly, I knew what we were going to do. Nobody wanted to say the first word, nor make the first move.

Great-Aunt broke the tense silence. "I will dump the pieces into the garbage bin after dark." She did not say what we all knew: as a lifelong worker, technically independent and separate from us children of capitalists, she was safe from attack. "Be careful," she added. "The Red Guards will not let you off easily. Do what you must and let me know when you're finished." She returned to her room and waited there.

"All right," Number 1 said, "one painting for each. Number 2 will be home soon to help."

I had little sense of what an antique was, but I loved the paintings, their beauty, power and poetic calligraphy. Now here we were ready to cut them into strips with scissors, as if we were doing some sort of craft work. I chose "Winter," thinking that my dislike of the cold damp season would make my task easier. But I was wrong. Soon tears fell onto the painting as I worked. I looked over at my baby sister, struggling with a pair of oversize scissors, scraping holes here and there in "Summer," and my tears came faster.

"Stop, you're ruining it!" I yelled, immediately realizing the stupidity of my words. I took her into my arms as she wept.

The last time we had all cried like this was when Mother died, eight months earlier.

"Go on," Number 1 urged. "Hurry!" Once more we set about our horrible task.

Seeing Great-Aunt leave, her sewing bag full, while my two brothers swept the wall with dirty brooms to hide the marks left by the pictures, my fear intensified. Any indication of a new paint job would lead to accusations of trying to hide evidence.

Our building was one of the few in the lane that had not yet been searched. Granny Ningbo was utterly terrified, jumping at every footstep. The Guards had hacked off Granny Yao's hair in Building 45, making her look like a crazy woman, and she was under close watch by her three grandchildren, for she had already tried to kill herself. Mrs. Qiao was in even worse shape after having talked back to the Red Guards when one of them insulted her children: the Guards had shaved half her hair off, creating what they mockingly called a yin-yang style. In the Ye family apartment, we waited for the inevitable.

At last, one hot night soon after, we heard footsteps on our stairs, followed by a knocking on our door. There were no gongs or drums, no yelling of slogans or insults. Tentatively, Number 1 pulled the door open. It was Uncle Yu, a worker from Father's factory, whom Father had employed as a cook years before because he was from Wuxi and could prepare the kind of food Father liked. Uncle Yu pressed his index finger to his lips and quickly shut the door.

He was a short, plump man, with a chubby, youthful face, though he was over fifty.

"Ah Du," he whispered to Number 1, "I came to warn you children. I overheard the Red Guards talking at the factory. They plan to raid your house tomorrow."

He went on to explain that all across the city, workers had split into two factions: the Loyalists, who still supported the city government, and the Shanghai Workers Revolutionary Rebels, who wanted to overthrow it. In his workplace, Number 2 had joined the Loyalists, for no one was allowed to stay neutral. Uncle Yu went on to tell us in hushed, apologetic tones that there were a number of *da-zi-bao* in Father's factory calling him insulting names and saying that his ghost refused to leave the place.

"The Communists claim there's no such thing as a ghost," I said, "so what are they doing, putting up such stupid posters?"

"Why are they coming here, Uncle Yu?" Number 3 cut in.

The old man looked as troubled as we felt. "I have no idea. But don't give anyone an excuse to hurt you." He pulled open the door, glanced out into the hall, and slipped away.

All of us were touched by Uncle Yu's courage. Out of loyalty to Father, he had put himself at great risk to warn us. That was the last time we saw this kind old man. After vindictive Red Guards revealed that his daughter had been adopted, she left Shanghai, taking Uncle Yu's grandchildren with her. He killed himself a few months later.

That night I could not sleep. Neither could Great-Aunt, who tossed and sighed beside me in the heat. She had said nothing after Uncle Yu left. When I thought about it, I realized she had been uncharacteristically silent since the raids had begun.

All her life Great-Aunt had made a living by her own hands. She had envied Mother and others like her who were also country girls but had lived a better life through a good marriage. While she herself had been cursed with bad luck, Great-Aunt had watched Mother start a new life, surrounded by children. Now, ironically, her bad luck had made her safe from attack.

We waited all the next day, all six of us huddled in our three-room apartment, and when dusk fell our building was hit a double score. Granny Ningbo's place was raided first. Then, after half an hour of shouting and crashing, it was our turn.

The insistent banging on our door was accompanied by bawled orders to open up. Seven people burst into the room— six Red Guards, two female and four male, all in their late teens or early twenties, all sporting the sinister red armbands. With them was a young guy from Father's factory. The leader, who was from Beijing, ordered us into my parents' bedroom.

"Form a line!" he shouted. We stood with heads bowed as he read us several quotations from Mao's treasure book.

"Whoever lives in this society is branded by the class he or she was born into!" one of the women Guards exclaimed when he had finished.

The Beijinger and the worker sat at Father's desk and examined our *hu-kou*—registration book—checking against a list in his hand and ordering us to stand still, face forward, and answer as our names were called. The Beijinger, about the same age as Number 1, had puffy red cheeks. His interrogation was continually interrupted by shouts from the other Guards, who had fanned out and begun a systematic search of our two rooms. Great-Aunt's room was left alone once the worker pointed out that she was a retired working-class woman. She remained inside with the door closed.

One of the women searching a dresser waved a pair of cotton socks with frequently mended soles and jeered, "Are these socks or shoes? It seems this family has iron soles!"

The Guards scouring the bedroom burst into laughter, but our interrogator kept his attention on his list. I stood silently, thinking of one of Mao's quotations: "The poorer people are, the better revolutionaries they will be." Another of his famous lines said that poverty was like a piece of new white paper on which one could write the finest calligraphy and draw the most beautiful pictures. Yet at the same time we were humiliated, first because we were the offspring of a capitalist, second because we were so poor we walked in mended socks.

A sudden movement interrupted my thoughts as the Beijinger pounded his fist on the desk.

"I knew it! I knew it!" he crowed. "Reactionaries are never straightforward in their evil ways. Look, everyone!" he shouted, bringing the ransacking of our meagre belongings to a temporary halt. "See what I have found."

He stood and strutted around the desk, pushing his finger into Number 2's face. "Tell me your name again."

"Ye Zhong-xing," answered my brother, his voice shaking.

"How old are you?"

"Eighteen."

"And you?" He pointed to Number 1.

"Ye Zheng-xing. Twenty."

"You see!" he looked around at his comrades and then suddenly punched Number 2 on the shoulder as he hissed, "Now you can tell me how your dead father was a supporter of the Guomindang reactionaries!"

I was dumbfounded. Beside me, Number 3 caught her breath. The guard was referring to the old government led by Chiang Kai-shek. Father had never supported him.

"We all know that Chiang Kai-shek's other name, given by his mother, is Chiang Zhong-zheng, the one he prefers but doesn't deserve!"

Number 1's name, Zheng—Upright—is a good name for a boy, though uncommon. Number 2's, Zhong, means Steadfast. These were names a scholar like my father would think appropriate for his male children.

But there was something wrong with the Red Guard's theory. "That can't be true," I spoke up, earning a warning glance from my eldest brother. "As you said, Chiang's name is Zhong-zheng. If Father had been a Nationalist sympathizer he would have named Number 1 Zhong instead of Number 2. The word order is wrong!"

"Shut up!" screamed the Guard, spit flying from his mouth. "That just shows your ghost-father's cunning! He reversed the order to fool people. But our Red Guards' eyes are much sharper, thanks to Mao Ze-dong Thought!"

I felt helpless in the face of his twisted logic. I had never so much as seen a photo of Chiang Kai-shek. The caricatures in our textbooks depicted a skinny, stiff man wearing a crossed bandage on his right temple. The Guomindang was described as rotten to its roots; Chiang Kai-shek's army had been full of "playboys" and all his soldiers had "rabbit legs" because they constantly ran away from battle during the wars against Japan and the Communists.

Our apartment pulsated with booming voices as the Red Guards began to vilify my father, shouting his name in unison, "Down with Ye Rong-ting! Down with the Guomindang running-dog, Ye Rong-ting!"

Despite everything, I couldn't help smiling inwardly at the fools shrieking around me. The literal translation of "down with" in Chinese—*da-dao*—is to knock someone down physically. They seemed to forget that my father was already in his grave.

As if reading my thoughts, the fools changed the chant. "Ten thousand deaths will not expiate Ye Rong-ting's crime! Feed his dead body to the dogs! And the dogs won't want it because it stinks too much!"

I stole a glance at my brothers and sisters. Their eyes were wide with fear. We had been badly enough off as children of the hated capitalist class; now the blood of a traitor supposedly ran in our veins. Yet, despite all the vindictive yelling and screaming, I felt strangely calm. The anxiety and panic of the past weeks and the endless waiting for the dreaded raid were over. Number 5, though, was shaking in terror, and I put my arm around her shoulders. I glanced at the door of Great-Aunt's room but it remained closed and there was no sound from within. Our neighbours, who in the past would always stick their noses into our apartment at the slightest provocation, were silent, as if they had suddenly lost their hearing.

When the shouting died down, Number 1 began to speak. Calmly he tried to reason with the Guards, telling them how my father's step-cousins had left for Taiwan before the liberation, but Father had remained. Why would he stay in Shanghai if he were a running-dog of Chiang Kai-shek?

"Aha, an overseas relationship!" one of the Guards exclaimed.

"Having illicit relations with foreign countries!" piped a second.

Another stupidity, I thought. Even at fourteen I knew clearly China's stern policy that Taiwan was a province of China. It was strictly prohibited to refer to it as a foreign country and the punishment for violation ranged from "reforming through labour" to imprisonment.

"But we have no contact with—"

"Shut up, traitor!" yelled the Beijing Red Guard.

"Make them change their names!" a thin woman with a long face and protruding teeth suggested. The rest of the Guards shouted agreement.

While the search resumed, my brothers were given five minutes to think of new names. One male Guard approached the Beijinger and presented him with a thick sheaf of papers.

"You can have them if you want," Number 1 offered without delay. "We don't want them."

"These are stock certificates and government bonds. Capitalist trash. Destroy them," the Beijinger sneered, handing them over to Number 1.

Without hesitation my brother tore the securities to bits while three of the Red Guards nodded their approval. As far as I was concerned the fancily printed bonds and certificates, the expropriation payments for Father's factory, were useless, just stacks of paper gathering dust in a drawer for years. The Red Guards, who thought the documents were valuable, praised Number 1's actions.

"Please," Number 2 spoke up. "I'd like to change my name to Loyalty." The character for loyalty was turning up more and more in *da-zi-bao* on walls and in store windows. The Red Guards accepted it right away. Number 2's choice was brilliant, because his new name—Zhong—was a homonym for "steadfast," his original name.

The Red Guards were starting to lose interest. Our two rooms offered nothing of note or value except a few items of furniture. But they did confiscate our family photos, claiming that they were "of the Four Olds" because in one grandfather had on an old-style "half melon" hat and in others Father wore a Western-style suit coat and tie and Mother had permed hair and makeup. Led by the Beijinger, the Red Guards left, chanting slogans as they thumped down the stairs and into the sky-well. Again I smiled inwardly. They had forgotten that Number 1 had not changed his name.

No one said a word. Number 5 wept quietly, shoulders hunched, hands shaking. Number 3 stood apart with her hands crossed on her chest, eyes wide. My two brothers looked at each other and nodded. We had survived.

After a few moments, Great-Aunt shuffled from her room, looking sheepish and guilty, but none of us blamed her for failing to come out and stick up for us. We all knew that would only have made things bad for her and worse for us. She immediately set about making tea and preparing us a late supper, which we ate in silence.

Over the next few weeks, trucks came into our lane and left loaded with goods—sofas, paintings, silk hangings, clothes, record players and records, even some cooking utensils—all were labelled "bourgeois" and appropriated by the Red Guards. What could not be seen was the jewellery and money they confiscated. And what they couldn't take away with them, they wrecked, leaving smashed roof tiles, holed walls, splintered floorboards and ripped chairs and chesterfields.

I realized then how wise Number 1 had been in voluntarily tearing up the securities. And I smiled whenever I thought about Number 2, whom Great-Aunt called slow and stubborn, brilliantly choosing his new name.

CHAPTER SIX

—

Mid-September brought disturbing reports from Beijing. In Tiananmen Square, another massive Red Guard rally had been reviewed by Chairman Mao and Lin Biao, minister of national defense, who had praised the Guards' nationwide beatings, lootings and burnings. "The direction of your action has always been correct," Lin Biao said. He applauded their revolutionary battles against "reactionary scholastic authorities," "bourgeois bloodsuckers" and "capitalist roaders who operated in a socialist environment but took the capitalist path in their thinking and policies." His words were a signal telling them whom to attack next.

Within a week the Red Guards' assaults had veered in the new direction, aiming at capitalist roaders. Families in our lane whose goods had been put under seal to be hauled away waited for weeks, but the trucks didn't arrive. The guards had lost interest and moved on to the new victims. Some of the braver neighbours began to unpack their "confiscated" belongings.

Meanwhile the railway station in downtown Shanghai was jammed with trains from other provinces, each car crammed with enthusiasts who had come to "exchange revolutionary experience" in a city they would otherwise never have had a chance to visit. These interlopers demanded free food and accommodation as well as unrestricted access to public buses, school campuses, office buildings and even some private homes. Neighbourhood committees supplied thousands of steamed buns to the young travellers. At the same time the Red Guards from Shanghai boarded every available train and ship bound for Beijing, leaving passengers who had bought their tickets stranded in stations and on docks because the Guards always had priority. The city authorities met every request laid down by the Guards, for fear of being branded capitalist roaders.

With Mao and Lin Biao fanning the flames, the Cultural Revolution burned like a wildfire out of control. Authorities in offices and factories who had provided the Red Guards with information on the class backgrounds of their employees now found themselves sweeping floors and scraping out toilets with those they had helped to denounce. Abandoning their livestock and neglecting their crops, peasants flooded into the cities demanding bonuses and benefits. The supply of produce in our local market dwindled and I was afraid that the "three hungry years," when I was eight to eleven, would return. While the rest of us idled at home because classes had been cancelled,

Number 2 fought in pitched battles against Rebels who had vowed to seize power from the city government. All across the city, factory production declined rapidly.

In mid-October I walked to school to collect my monthly ¥9 welfare allowance, worried that the collapse of the school system might interrupt my stipend.[7] Except for a few girls skipping in the yard, there was nothing going on. Nervously, I entered the office and asked the accountant, a pleasant, gray-haired woman in her fifties, about my stipend.

"Don't worry, Xiao Ye, the teachers are still getting paid even though there are no classes, so why shouldn't you get your welfare allowance?"

As she counted out the cash she added, her voice low, "Did you hear? Poor Old Uncle Zhang's ashes are still in a box in the shed where he hanged himself. No one has claimed them."

Old Uncle Zhang was not the only one. In those days there were many suicides. I was shocked by the way my neighbours gossiped about them in public. They sounded as if they were telling a thrilling story or describing a scene from the movies. Big Fatty, who lived below us, calmly related one day that he had almost become a "cushion for a flying-down person" who had thrown himself from a high-rise on Nanjing Road. Bloated corpses were regularly fished out of the Huangpu River; people gassed themselves; others jumped from high

---

[7] For anyone enrolled in middle school or university, welfare payments were administered by the institution rather than the neighbourhood committee.

windows, leaving their blood and guts hanging on window frames or ledges that projected from the buildings.

All suicides were condemned by the authorities as "alienating oneself from the Party and the people." The papers announced that the victims deserved to be dead, and the messier the death, the better. At fourteen I could hardly imagine what would drive a person to take her own life. But I would soon learn.

Even though the new political wind had put capitalist roaders at the top of the hate list, thus pushing bourgeois families like ours to second place, I was still shocked when Number 1 announced one evening that he and seven other students at the university had formed a musical band, the Spreading Mao Ze-dong Thought Group, and planned to go to Beijing. "We've even made ourselves red armbands," he added, his eyes dancing.

Their choice of name, he explained, would keep them safe from harm. All of them were from capitalist families, so calling themselves Red Guards was strictly forbidden. But the name of their band was ideal. It echoed the posters seen everywhere: "Making Mao Ze-dong Thought known to everyone and every household is a sacred duty of each Chinese citizen."

He had somehow managed to save his clarinet from the fire at the university—Western musical instruments were destroyed by the Guards—and that night I heard him practising out on the terrace. The clarinet stopped; and he started to sing.

The vast universe and boundless land
Are not as great as the kindness of the
*   Communist Party.*
The love of your mother and father
Is not as deep as that of Chairman Mao
*   for you.*

"How can you utter those disgusting words after all we've been through?" I yelled through the open window. "What has Chairman Mao's love done for us?"

Number 3 rushed over and dragged me away. "Are you out of your mind, Ah Si? Someone might hear you! Why are you angry at him? They're just songs, empty words. They don't mean any more than anything else nowadays. Come on, you'll get us all in trouble."

That was typical of my elder sister. Nothing mattered to her as long as the sky didn't fall down. Number 1 left for Beijing the next day with his clarinet hidden in his bag.

At home, life was dull, the days long and uneventful. Only Number 2 and Great-Aunt came and went. There was no school to attend, no homework to do. We three girls were too young to attend the neigbourhood meetings with Great-Aunt, and because of the factional wars, the streets were dangerous and unpredictable. Libraries and movie houses, which we couldn't afford to go to in any case, had been shut down. Even the radio offered no relief—only incessant propaganda announcements echoing the bulletins that blasted from loudspeakers mounted on poles along our lane.

We received no news from Number 1, even after a few weeks. I was worried about him—he was not street-smart—but I envied him his adventure. Desperate for something to do, I asked Great-Aunt to teach me needlepoint. I slept late in the mornings and took naps each afternoon.

Beijing continued to be a sea of political turmoil, with rallies so massive that they had to be divided between Tiananmen Square and the capital airport while Mao, along with his wife, Jiang Qing, and Lin Biao, shuttled back and forth to review the throngs of Red Guards from every province. Hearing all this, I felt even more envious. All those Red Guards—some the same age as me—were able to travel to Beijing for free, and to see the country along the way. Never having travelled farther than my grandfather's house near Wuxi, I fantasized about taking the train to Beijing and visiting the palaces and temples I had heard so much about in school.

Late one night at the beginning of November, about three weeks after Number 1 left, I heard someone calling my name from the lane. "Ah Si, Ah Si." Then another voice. "Ye Tingxing!"

Great-Aunt sat up, startled. "The Red Guards!" she whispered. "What do they want?"

She scrambled out of bed and tottered on her bound feet to the window, throwing it open. Terrified, I squeezed in beside her, peering down into the darkness. I was barely able to make out two girls from my school, Xiu-fang and Guo-zheng, standing in the backdoor lane.

"I know them," I said, relieved. "They're all right."

Both girls were members of the Red Guard sub-unit in my school. We had not been close before the Cultural Revolution, but circumstances had given us something in common and they were among the few who had not been hostile to me.

I headed out of our apartment and downstairs before Great-Aunt had a chance to object, and as soon as I opened the back door, Xiu-fang said excitedly, "We thought you might want to come with us." Each of them had a small bundle slung over her shoulder. "We're on our way to the railway station to catch a train to Beijing," said Guo-zheng.

I pulled them inside and closed the door. "How can I go to Beijing if I'm not even allowed to use the front gate at school?" I asked, knowing that you had to be "pure" to make the pilgrimage to the capital.

"There aren't many Red Guards at the station at this time of night," said Guo-zheng, pulling strips of red cloth from her pocket. "We can wear these until we get on the train. As soon as we are out of Shanghai, we'll be just as good as anyone else. Who'll know what our parents used to be?"

"Brilliant!" I exclaimed, excitement surging through me. I poked Guo-zheng's bundle. "What do you have in here?"

"Not much. My winter stuff and a change of clothes. My mother said it's much colder in Beijing."

Mention of her mother made me remember I had left Great-Aunt standing by her window. How could I persuade her?

"Come upstairs," I said, "but wait for me in the hall."

Great-Aunt was sitting up in bed, and as soon as I entered the room she gave me a look that was only too familiar—the corners of her eyes curved downwards at the same degree as her mouth. Ignoring her scowl, I took a direct approach.

"Great-Aunt, I am going to Beijing. I am going no matter what you say."

"Is that what they are here for?" she shouted. "Are they missing an arm or a leg that they need you to help them travel? Or are they anxious to see *you* lose one of *your* limbs?"

Her outcry brought my two sisters rushing. "What's the matter?" Number 3 cried. "Have the Red Guards come back?"

"Your foolish sister wants to join them! She wants to go to Beijing! With two other brainless girls!"

Number 3 grabbed me by the shoulders and shook me hard. "Which one of your bones is itching, Ah Si?"

"I know where you should go," Number 5 piped up. "To the hospital, to get your head examined. Have you forgotten what Number 1 told us? It isn't safe for us to go out."

"And where is Number 1 now?" I countered. "Beijing, that's where!"

The arguments that followed brought to mind the scene when the five of us saw Auntie Yi-feng, my mother's sister, off at the bus stop after Mother's funeral. We couldn't afford even one train ticket to Wuxi, so Mother had had none of her children by her side when she was put into the ground. Now, here I was, able to travel all the way to Beijing with no need to pay a cent.

Great-Aunt began to recycle the washing-area gossip—the turmoil in the streets, the beatings, the suicides—in an attempt to scare my decision out of my head. She refused to provide me with winter clothes, warning that I would freeze to death in the frigid northern city she had never visited.

"That will be just fine with me," I told her stubbornly. "People in Beijing will not allow me to freeze to death. Didn't your newspaper readers tell you that the student-pilgrims are treated royally, as Chairman Mao's guests?"

To support my point I called in Guo-zheng and Xiu-fang, who had been cooling their heels in the hall. Ignoring the embarrassed looks on their faces, I pointed at them. "Ask them if I need to take anything with me." Guo-zheng's mouth opened, then closed again without a sound. "You don't think their parents would let them go if it isn't safe, do you?" I argued, knowing I had scored a hit.

My two sisters fell silent as Great-Aunt got out of bed and hobbled to her dresser, saying nothing. That was typical of her. She knew that silence was the best medicine for my temper. When I saw her remove her long woolen scarf and a pair of wool gloves from a drawer I instantly wished I could take back everything I had said, even half of it, or that she would criticize my impertinence. I had never in my life acted like this, full of denial and allowing no discussion.

My eyes followed her every move, hoping she would ask me to help her. Silently she squeezed past me to the attic, where we stored our winter clothes. Number 3 helped her up the ladder. She let me stew in my own juice as she packed, playing her best game on me. Finally she spoke.

"Ah Si, take off your undershirt so I can sew a pocket on it."

She put a five-yuan note into the pocket along with some special food coupons that could be used anywhere in the country and secured it with two large safety pins. Normal coupons could be used only in the locality where they were issued, a measure to keep people from moving outside their designated area.

"Don't ever take this shirt off," she warned. "And use the money and coupons only when necessary." She then took out her purse and gave me some small money and local food coupons. "Buy some bread at the train-station store in case you can't get food when you're travelling."

If anyone at that moment had said so much as a word to persuade me to stay I would have called the whole thing off. I had won the argument but didn't want the reward. Ashamed as I was, I would have traded anything for a hug from Great-Aunt. But it didn't happen. I couldn't remember a single occasion when Great-Aunt showed me any physical affection, though I knew she had deep feelings for me. Showing emotion even among family members was criticized as non-proletarian.

As I said goodbye to Great-Aunt and my sisters, I pledged to myself that as soon as I arrived in Beijing I would jump on a return train. I missed them already and held back tears, determined they would not see me cry. In the lane, I walked backwards until the windows of our apartment disappeared.

CHAPTER SEVEN

—

The North Station square was almost empty, washed with pale fluorescent light, forbidding and cold. Boldly we marched into the unguarded waiting room, passed the long rows of benches occupied by hundreds of sleeping men, women and children, and made our way to the platform. There the scene was totally different. People milled around in a hubbub. Loudspeakers pumped out train numbers, schedules and advice to travellers. Passengers hung out of train windows talking to others on the platform. No wonder the streets and the square are empty, I thought: everyone is here.

Guo-zheng stopped. She fished in her pocket and pulled out three red armbands. "Here, let's put these on now before we get to the train."

Mine said *Hong Wei Dong*—Red Defending the East, a suitably ambiguous slogan. East symbolized Chairman Mao, from the song "The East Is Red." I pocketed the black band I still wore to mourn my mother. The less personal information, the better.

We pushed our way along the platform, searching for the Beijing train, but were unable to find it. Every train was so packed that the doors could not be opened. The passengers seemed to have set up camp in the cars. Heads protruded from windows. Some people busily brushed their teeth, spitting onto the tracks, which were littered with garbage. A few of the trains had been stranded in the station for days because the railway lines were all blocked, particularly north of Nanjing on the Beijing line. The railroad was trying in vain to accommodate the mammoth flow of traffic to the capital, as factional wars among the railroad workers added to the chaos. Their posters covered the walls of the station. Some were even glued to the ceilings.

We continued to stroll around, now willing to take any train so long as it was heading north. We found one and begged the passengers to let us in through the windows. Some rejected us, telling us there was no room, even the aisles were full. Some asked us to fetch fresh water as the price of entry, then refused us after we had complied. We were not strong enough to force our way in and, being very small for my age, I had to stand on my toes just to reach the windowsill of the train. The air was punctuated by screams as people attempted to climb through the narrow windows, which were no bigger than one foot high and two feet wide.

Xiu-fang's constant complaining got on my nerves. By this time I wanted nothing more than to go to sleep. When we all sat down around one of the pillars, I put my head on my knees and drifted off.

"Ah Si, wake up!" I awoke, startled, cold and disoriented, and heard a shrill whistle nearby. I jumped to my feet and looked at the clock above the platform. It was four o'clock in the morning.

"A train is leaving!" Guo-zheng too jumped up. Suddenly the area became a war zone as those around us snatched up their belongings and surged toward the departing train.

"Quick! This is our chance!" Guo-zheng shouted above the din, pointing to a stationary train on the other side of the platform. Passengers were rushing out of its coaches and heading for the moving train.

Xiu-fang crouched down and I got onto her shoulders. When she struggled to her feet, lifting me higher, I was clutched by hands stretched from the window, then turned horizontal and passed like a small plank into the train. My two schoolmates were hauled in after me.

We found ourselves in a car jammed to the walls with bodies. All the benches were full, the aisles were blocked with seated passengers, people lay in the spaces under the seats. The only space left for me was the luggage rack. I climbed up and lay on my back, my face inches from the curved ceiling. The train was hot, the air a stew of odours: unwashed bodies, cigarette smoke, urine. Wrinkling my nose and reflecting that Great-Aunt would have a fit in this fetid air, I made a pillow of my bundle and fell asleep.

When I awoke it was light, and the train was in motion. I panicked, unaware of where I was, and banged my head. Stars spun before my eyes.

"We're moving!" I yelled. "Where are we?"

"Why shouldn't we be moving?" a gruff voice below me responded. "We're in a train." Laughter followed. "We'll be in Wuxi soon."

Wuxi! I lay back, staring at the ceiling, and began to think. I was already so homesick I would gladly have jumped down from the train and walked back home. Then a thought struck me. Why couldn't I get off the train at Wuxi and make my way to my grandparents' house in Qingyang? I could visit my parents' grave. I hadn't seen my grandparents for more than seven mostly bad years.

Clutching the bars of the luggage rack and poking my head downwards, I caught the attention of an older, tough-looking girl sitting next to the window.

"Is it possible to get off at Wuxi station?"

"Why?" she frowned at me. "Don't you want to go to Beijing and see Chairman Mao?"

Her tone of voice and red armband reminded me of the purpose of my mission. My instinct warned me to be careful.

"Of course," I said. "But I understand this train is only going to Nanjing and—"

"So? That doesn't mean we can't get to Beijing." She stood up and looked at me closely, her voice softer. "How old are you? Are you travelling alone?"

"Fourteen," I answered. "I am in the third year of middle school."

"I'm seventeen, from Yang Pu District. Which district are you from?"

"Jing An. I'm from Ai Guo Girls' School."

I felt someone tapping my feet. It was Guo-zheng, who glared meaningfully. Yang Pu was a working-class district. Most of its residents originally came from Su Bei, a poverty-stricken section of Jiangsu Province, and were looked down upon by other Shanghainese. This girl would thus be a genuine Red Guard, not a pretender like me. I had blabbed that I came from Jing An District, an area full of people with bad class background. No wonder Guo-zheng had tried to shut me up. All troubles came from the mouth, Great-Aunt would have said.

"Yes, I have heard of your district." I wished I had bumped my head harder so I wouldn't have started this conversation.

"I want to trade places with you," Guo-zheng interrupted.

I climbed down, stepped across the seat backs and was directed to the rack across the aisle. Obviously moving me was Guo-zheng's way of shutting me up. I would not tell her of my plan to get off the train far short of our destination.

—

If it had not been for the sign, I would never have recognized Wuxi station, even though I had seen it many times in my early childhood. As we drew slowly to a halt people swarmed onto the platform and began to pound at the doors and windows, screaming that they wanted to get in. The chaotic scene frightened me. Nobody dared to open the windows, even though, with the train still and no ventilation, the coach became so stifling that it was difficult to draw a breath. To open the window would be like punching a hole in a dike. I changed my plan, horrified at the thought of trying to climb down into that desperate crowd, and made up my mind to stop in Wuxi on my way back from Beijing.

An hour or so later, the besieged train shuddered and began to inch its way out of the station. I dozed the rest of the afternoon away and it was almost dark when we reached Nanjing. The railway workers told us to get out. It was the end of the line and the train needed to be serviced.

Guo-zheng, Xiu-fang and I decided to stick around the station rather than follow the other pilgrims into the city to see the sights, rest in free accommodations and eat free meals. We were joined by the girl I had spoken to earlier. She called herself Yang-yang—Bright Sun—a stylish name at the time. Her father had originally named her Zhao Di—Waiting for Brothers. Compared with me, she was tall, at least five-foot-eight, and three times heavier.

Before I did anything else I had to visit the washroom. The four of us pushed through the wall of clamorous travellers, and when we finally made it, I discovered one of the unpleasant results of hundreds of thousands of human beings in a confined space. Unlike most public bathrooms, this one was large, with one sink and two rows of cubicles separated from one another by waist-high walls. The "toilet" was a wide slot in the floor, periodically sluiced by water that flowed under all the cubicles and emptied into a cistern. There was no water in the tap in this stinking and fly-infested place and every toilet was plugged by a pile of human dung that rose above the level of the floor, which was wet with urine. When I stepped carefully into a cubicle, I gagged at the sight and the putrid smell. But desperate times call for desperate measures.

Back outside, we walked along the rails beside the coaches, begging entry to the northbound train, bribing the occupants with what little food we had and fetching water for them. At last we met a sympathetic Red Guard who helped drag me in through the window after Yang-yang lifted me up. But Xiu-fang was heavy and clumsy, and after numerous pushings and pullings she fell in a heap onto the track, screaming in pain and clutching her right ankle.

One of the passengers gave Guo-zheng directions to the station's clinic. I tried to climb down to help her with Xiu-fang.

"No, no. You stay," Guo-zheng shouted up to me. "Keep a place for us when we get back."

She returned half an hour later, but without Xiu-fang. After Yang-yang and I had hauled her in through the window, she gave us her report.

"The doctor said Xiu-fang has to have her ankle X-rayed because it's probably broken. He assured me that the clinic will treat her as one of Chairman Mao's guests."

It was far past midnight when our train was severed into parts and shunted onto the ferry for the ride across the Yangtze River. By then I had stretched out on the luggage rack. When dawn broke, I awoke to find we were still in Jiangsu Province. By then my feet had swelled so badly my shoelaces had burst and the coach was so crowded I could not climb down to relieve the pressure.

Yang-yang became our kindly big sister. Her long legs and strong arms served us well. When the train stopped at a station, she would jump down onto the platform, fetch water for us and collect a few of the steamed buns the locals had made to show their support for the Red Guards. Whenever she praised me in front of the other passengers, calling me a "tiny pea full of mountain-high revolutionary spirit and iron determination to see Chairman Mao," I felt guilty, for I had lied to her, telling her my parents were workers at Number 13 Textile Factory near our home. Flat on my back on the hardwood racks, I wondered if I would spend the rest of my life telling fibs.

I began to lose track of time on the slow, endless journey, frequently interrupted by stops. Every part of my body ached. My pigtails had absorbed the odour of urine in the car and I feared I would never be able to wash my hair clean again. At long last the train drew to a halt and someone yelled, "We're here! We're in Beijing!"

A deafening cheer followed and people began to gather their belongings, bumping and banging into one another in pandemonium. For the first time I was glad to be up on the racks, above the crush. Windows were thrown up. Bundles were tossed out, followed by bodies, crawling, jumping, falling from the train. But there were no gongs and drums to greet us as I had expected.

It was shortly after midnight, and Yang-yang, practical as always, suggested we stay on the train until morning. But the train workers ordered us off, telling us that soldiers were wait-ing to take us to our destination. We were not in the centre depot as I had thought, but in the southern suburb, at the sta-tion called Yong Ding Men—Gate of Lasting Permanence. But I was in Beijing! I tried not to think about the irony that it was the hated Cultural Revolution that had given me the opportunity for unpaid travel to the ancient capital, a place I might otherwise never have seen.

CHAPTER EIGHT

—

For the first time in our journey, I used the door of the train. Shivering in the cold, I made my way through the station with my friends, exhausted, hungry and aching in every limb, my laceless cotton shoes flapping on the pavement. Outside stood long lines of army men, silent in their green greatcoats and hats with long earflaps.

We marched to a nearby park where we stood a long time in the dark, some jumping up and down to keep warm, until army trucks arrived to carry us away and deposit us before a complex of large, mostly unlit buildings. There we were herded into a spacious, dimly lit room, and instructed to sleep on the floor. I did so gladly.

I dreamt I was at my school, standing before a brick wall under the relentless midday sun. But I awoke to find myself wrapped in a blanket, fully clothed in my cotton-padded pants and coat with Great-Aunt's knitted wool scarf around my head and neck. I was sandwiched between two shapeless forms, motionless under green blankets.

"Yang-yang? Guo-zheng?" I whispered, shaking the body beside me.

The figure turned my way, revealing a round face, puffy eyes and a sharp chin from which a few long hairs protruded. I scrambled to my feet in terror. I had been sleeping with a man! I looked around in a panic. I knew nothing about where babies came from—except that even as a child I understood the significance of men and women "sleeping together." I had overheard adults' conversations and had listened as kids at school related stories in which rape was referred to as "sleeping with flower girls." Babies were the result. I had never asked Great-Aunt for details because I knew she would not provide them and I dared not ask others for fear of being accused of having dirty thoughts, the worst kind of criticism for a girl. So I had pictured the process as some kind of chemical reaction, like the one I studied in physics where a dog salivated when shown food. Was I pregnant now?

Terrified, I yelled for Yang-yang and Guo-zheng. All over the room heads popped up; eyes stared; angry voices shushed me.

"I'm sorry," I announced to no one in particular as I stepped over the sleeping forms between me and my friends, dragging my blanket. After a few moments of whispering, they calmed me down.

A little while later an officer strode into the warehouse. People's Liberation Army officers—the PLA included all the armed forces, not just the army—did not distinguish themselves from enlisted personnel by wearing insignia, braided ropes, medals or epaulets. They had four pockets on their olive drab Sun Zhong-shan style jackets instead of two. This officer was in his thirties, tall and bulky, and when he spoke, a string of words rolled off his "tightly curved tongue," as southerners describe northerners' speech.

"What did you say?" I asked in my Shanghai-flavoured *pu-tòng-hua*.[8]

He smiled and spoke more slowly. We were in the compound of the General Political Department of the PLA, he said, and were requested to attend a meeting in the canteen across the basketball ground. Breakfast would be ready when we got there.

With my two friends I made my way across the courtyard toward the canteen, shadowed by the biggest buildings I had ever seen. A five-story structure was considered a high-rise in China. We were given two enamel bowls, one for hot rice gruel, the other for steamed buns. To my amazement I didn't have to show any identification to get my food. No money, no coupons were required. No wonder those around me stuffed themselves so full they could hardly walk. It reminded me of

---

[8.] *Pu-tong-hua*—Common Speech—became the official dialect of the whole country after the founding of the People's Republic in 1949. In North America it is known as Mandarin.

what I had learned at school about real communism: from each according to his ability, to each according to his need.

Cheered by the hot food, we listened as the officer formally welcomed us and then, inevitably, set down rules. Once we had participated in a rally, we must vacate the capital within forty-eight hours because of the overwhelming number of youngsters arriving in Beijing each day. We were here to "exchange revolutionary experiences," the officer admonished, not to sight-see and stuff ourselves with free food. Each of us was issued a free bus pass, good for the whole city.

I was overwhelmed by the feeling that, at fourteen, I was in control of my own life for the first time. Food and lodgings were free; I could go anywhere I wanted in our nation's capital, a place my parents had talked about but never seen. I decided to enjoy this freedom for as long as it lasted. Awed by my sense of independence and discovery, I walked out the gate with my two friends. It was a bright sunny day, but without an overcoat I was chilly, even in the sun. The streets, lined with leafless trees, seemed empty compared to crowded Shanghai.

Yang-yang said goodbye to me and Guo-zheng at the corner of Hongguang Road, originally called Baiguang Road. *Bai*—White—had been replaced by the favoured *Hong*—Red. All over China the Red Guards had renamed the streets. I had even heard stories about attempts to alter traffic lights so that red meant go and green meant stop.

Guo-zheng and I wanted to visit Tiananmen Square to see the Gate of Heavenly Peace, which was described in one of my nursery rhymes as "red brick walls and yellow glazed tiles; tall and gigantic, beautiful and magnificent." Hunching our shoulders against the chill, we followed the twists and turns of the alleyways and found ourselves on Changan Avenue. I felt like a fish swimming in a sea of red and yellow. The citizens of Beijing had responded to the call to make the capital a "sea of red" by writing Mao's quotations in red paint on a yellow background, plastering walls and buildings with slogans and exhortations. As I walked along past the roughly painted walls and hastily written slogans, I wondered whether people in the city had ever run out of red and yellow paint.

China's broadest and most elegant avenue was lined with leafless trees—and temporary latrines, constructed of bamboo poles with woven bamboo mats wired to them to the height of my head. Inside the bamboo enclosures, cement paving squares had been lifted and pits dug. These were the revolutionary toilets. When full, they were covered over with earth and the squares put back where they belonged. The area was slick with frozen urine. Millions of visiting Red Guards created more than just political problems.

The red walls of the Forbidden City were papered over with *da-zi-bao*. The Palace Museum itself was, to my disappointment, closed, because sightseeing was discouraged as unrevolutionary. Guo-zheng and I sat on the broad steps of the Great Hall of the People across the road and rested in the sun. Later, tired, we returned to the barracks.

Our newly assigned room had once been someone's office. Six bunks lined one wall. After another hot meal, the officer in charge called us to a meeting and asked us all to state our class background and report on our day's activity in the "heart city" of our country. I prepared myself to lie again when my turn came. I was stunned when one girl told the group that she was from a shopkeeper's family. How could she be so stupid? I thought. Surely she would have trouble heaped upon her?

But no one showed any resentment. I realized that here, too, the "capitalist roader" had taken over as the number-one class enemy. I began to relax a little, but lied anyway when it was my turn, reporting that I had spent the entire day closely studying the *da-zi-bao* on the walls of the Forbidden City.

Yang-yang, fervent as she was, read out the accusations she had copied down at Qinghua University. The most dramatic and shocking of these attacked Liu Shao-qi, president and second man after Chairman Mao. He was declared the number-one capitalist roader who aimed to change the nature of communism. Worse than all this political denunciation was the information from his private life.

According to Yang-yang's notes, Liu Shao-qi had married five times. She had written down the details of each failed marriage. There were even cartoons of Liu and his latest wife on the posters, Yang-yang reported. I listened, gaping, as she gave out information that until then had been treated almost as a military secret. Any gossip about the private life of our leaders was a sure road to severe criticism and punishment. It had been revealed only recently that Mao Ze-dong himself had a young wife named Jiang Qing and, although people were naturally curious about her, no one dared speculate about Mao's personal life.[9] Ordinary citizens like me lived in an environment where we had to reveal every detail of our personal and family history for several generations back, yet in this society where the word privacy did not exist, the impression had been given that state leaders led the life of nuns or monks. But if the president's life could now be turned inside out like a dirty sock, I wondered, who would be safe?

—

The afternoon following Yang-yang's scathing report, the women's bathhouses opened. It had been almost a week since I had washed in warm water and I rushed to line up. Two hours later, after a long shower in gloriously hot water, Guo-zheng and I decided to go out and have a treat: candied haw berries, famous in Beijing. My hair was still wet, and soon I had icicles clicking at my ears. I paid dearly for this foolishness. That night I developed a high fever and ran from one nightmare to another. My own screaming woke me up, and in the morning Guo-zheng fetched a doctor. My temperature was around forty degrees and I was taken to the infirmary on a stretcher.

If the plentiful food at the canteen was a luxury, the hospital was paradise. The ward was much brighter and cleaner than the one I had seen when visiting Mother at the hospital in Shanghai. There were five beds in the room besides mine, all filled. Mine

---

9. In fact, Jiang Qing was Mao's fourth wife.

was like a cloud. I lay on a spring mattress and bounced up and down on it. The nurses were friendly and kind, so different from people in the outside world, where it seemed to me that yelling and shouting filled our everyday lives.

When I had recovered several days later and began to eat again, I was even offered a choice of food. What an easy life! Great-Aunt would have said, "Hold out your arms and you will be dressed; open your mouth and you will be fed." At night we patients were entertained by a song and dance troupe.

One day after I had left the infirmary I learned at the evening meeting that there would be a big rally at the airport the next day. We would see Chairman Mao with our own eyes! Preparations must be made and, of course, new rules laid down.

First, we were paired up at random, each partner under the other's responsibility and scrutiny—a common surveillance technique. No one was allowed to leave the compound until the morning, when we would all depart for the rally together. No pocketknives or sharp metal tools were permitted. We were reminded how vast the crowd would be—hundreds of thousands. While marching we should never, ever try to pick up anything we had dropped, or we might never stand up again. Each of us was issued a pair of extra-long shoelaces and instructed on how to bind them tightly around our insteps, since the thousands of trampling feet around us might grind our heels and pull off our shoes. Not only would the lacing technique keep us from injury or even death, it would aid the street sweepers who usually faced mountains of lost shoes when the rally was over. On the way out of the canteen everyone was to be given a paper bag holding two boiled eggs and two fat steamed buns stuffed with pickled vegetables.

I couldn't believe I was going to see Chairman Mao in person! I had seen his picture all my life, staring at me from walls, buses and store windows. In real life I saw people aging or even dying, most of them much younger than Mao; but he, in my eyes, didn't seem real. He was like the immortals I read about in fairy tales, never one day older, with the same smile and the same mole under his mouth. The songs and slogans called him the sun, the rescuing star of our universe. Was he really a great man? Or was he the author of all our misfortunes as I had always believed? I wondered if my attitude would change after I saw him.

Before we were allowed to climb into the military trucks early the next morning, my partner and I, a girl from Anhui Province, searched each other in front of another pair, then reversed roles with them. After an hour's jouncing along the cold streets, we were dropped off about five kilometres from the airport and ordered to form ranks. We marched eight in a row under a cloudy sky, scrutinized by PLA soldiers and officers, singing our revolutionary songs. Even the fierce wind from the northwest didn't seem too bad. Compared to my night parade in Shanghai months before, this one was a picnic—and much more exciting.

Bright chalk lines divided the tarmac at the airport into squares. There wasn't an airplane in sight. Each square could hold at least thirty rows of twelve spectators. The sun was peeking from behind the clouds when we sat down, as instructed, on the icy cement, cross-legged, like the soldiers in front of us. Because I was small, I was put in the second row, so I was certain I'd get a good view. We were required to remain seated throughout the rally so everyone could see, and under no circumstances were we to rush the motorcade.

At noon, I broke out my food, peeling chilled eggs under the envious eyes of those who had eaten theirs earlier. Although the steamed buns were now hard as a rock, I didn't dare drink too much water to soften them. There were toilets, but they were far from us and no one knew exactly when Chairman Mao would appear.

It got colder. My bottom was like a block of ice and my legs grew numb. I received permission from a soldier in front of me to kneel to ease my cramped limbs. Hours of singing and reading from the red book crept by. I yawned and shifted my position, my enthusiasm dampened by boredom.

Suddenly, from far away, came the rumble of engines, then hysterical chanting—"Long live Chairman Mao!"—roared in the sky. One minute I was slapping my numb legs to warm them, the next I was rising to my feet, in spite of the orders not to, yelling at the top of my lungs like everyone else.

"Long live Chairman Mao!" I shouted, my voice lost in the waves of sound.

Tears streamed from my eyes. The motorcade was moving, bearing down on us. Peering between the soldiers in front of me, I got a brief glimpse of a jeep. There was Mao's wife, Jiang Qing! And Lin Biao standing right beside her! They were waving their red books, but their faces were pale and unsmiling. Frantically I searched for Chairman Mao. In another jeep I saw Liu Shao-qi, Mao's second-in-command, dressed in army fatigues, looking worn down and disturbed. I recalled what Yang-yang had told us about him. My eyes followed his grim form until it disappeared, and I wondered how such a powerful man could be attacked just like the teachers in my school and the neighbours in my lane back home.

It was then that I realized I had missed Chairman Mao!

I closed my eyes and covered my face with my hands, feeling cheated and lost.

On the way back through streets jammed with marching youngsters and loaded trucks, although exhausted from ten hours of walking and waiting in the cold, I hid my disappointment. Everyone was excited, telling each other how clearly they had seen Chairman Mao, how healthy he looked, how kind he appeared, how lucky they were. Some could not wait to get back to the barracks: they wrote down their impressions as the truck bounced through the streets, overwhelmed by the sense that they had participated in the making of history.

I joined them enthusiastically, using my imagination, unwilling to admit that I hadn't seen the Chairman at all, even though I had been in the second row. If everyone else had seen him, so had I. That was what I was going to say to everyone, including my siblings and Great-Aunt. That night when I told Guo-zheng that I had also seen Liu Shao-qi, she covered my mouth with her hand, fearing I would cause trouble again.

Yang-yang pointed out that he had been in the last jeep. We all knew what that meant: he had fallen from Mao's favour.

Early the next morning, after our last free meal, we were trucked to the train station. I had already changed my plan to stop at Wuxi. I never thought I could miss Great-Aunt so much.

CHAPTER NINE

—

January, the first anniversary of Mother's death, ushered in another year of turmoil. More state leaders were denounced and jailed, and Chairman Mao urged the whole nation to seize power from the capitalist roaders who "still occupied the bourgeois headquarters across the country." Confused as they were by Mao's inexact call to arms, the people of Shanghai took action. On January 4, the Shanghai Workers Revolutionary Rebels overthrew the municipal government, which had, so the radio broadcast told us, "turned rotten to its roots." The coup was headed by a textile-factory security officer named Wang Hong-wen under orders from Zhang Chun-qiao, who rose to be head of the Cultural Revolution Authority for the entire country. Jiang Qing—Mrs. Mao—and Wang and Zhang, joined by a well-known writer, Yao

Wen-yuan, later formed the notorious "Gang of Four."[10]

This "January Storm" in Shanghai brought great trouble to our doorstep. Number 2, being a member of the defeated Loyalist faction, was swept up in the subsequent purge.[11] The Shanghai Revolutionary Committee had received the blessing of Chairman Mao himself and it set about housecleaning with a vengeance. Soon the majority of Loyalists, after criticism and self-criticism, were identified as "good people but misled" due to their "simple but pure class feeling toward the Party." But that was not the case for Number 2. He was set up as an example of those who "secretly supported the old municipal government while showing their resentment of the Cultural Revolution led by our great Chairman Mao"—in other words, my brother was labelled anti-Mao, a deadly charge. He was forced to sweep the floor and scrub toilets alongside former factory authorities during the day and to submit to merciless condemnation at evening rallies. The cleaning during the day was actually easier than his job dyeing rubber, and he continued to receive his salary. It was the public humiliation of the "struggle meetings" and the constant fear that things could get worse for him that hurt most.[12]

[10.] The Gang of Four, claiming to represent Mao's wishes, was responsible for some of the worst excesses of the Cultural Revolution.

[11.] In a purge, opponents are removed from their positions and often killed.

[12.] A "struggle meeting" was an assembly held to condemn someone publicly and force him or her to admit errors or thought-crimes. Victims were often attacked physically and sometimes beaten to death. The main purpose of such meetings was to terrorize everyone, not just punish the so-called wrongdoers.

One night when he had been allowed to come home for clean clothes, I could tell that Number 2 was scared.

"Some people," he said, "have been beaten to death by their fellow workers in the struggle meetings, especially in factories involved in military projects."

I was horrorstruck. "You mean the same might happen to you?"

He shrugged his thin shoulders. "I don't know."

The Red Terror ushered in the spring. Fighting among the factions broke out everywhere, each group claiming to be more revolutionary than the next. Factories, government offices, research institutions and communes had turned into battlegrounds of hatred. The streets on the outskirts of Shanghai rang with gunfire. The history I learned at school was no longer a theoretical study: the Communists' struggle to eliminate all classes other than proletarians had escalated. Chairman Mao continuously harangued us that this last fight was *Ni-si-wo-huo*—You die; I live. The bare fists and bronze belt buckles used by the Red Guards were now replaced by iron rods, steel bars and bullets. The entire nation was in an uproar, and cruelty ruled.

And then Chairman Mao did what many thought he would never do. Until now the PLA had remained neutral, kept out of the Cultural Revolution. But when Mao was notified that in some areas of the country the rebels had not been successful, while in others the fighting was out of control, he relented and ordered in the army. The army's involvement made the muddy waters muddier. And it brought

Commander-in-Chief Lin Biao into prominence as Mao's number-two man.

Was this how I would have to spend the rest of my life— hiding at home, fearing for the safety of myself and my family, watching my future dissolve? The days dragged by, but my sleep was filled with nightmares, especially when Number 2 was forced to fight in the streets again, for the PLA had at last moved into Shanghai to oust a powerful faction in the Shanghai Diesel Engine Factory. The battle raged for three days. This time, the losers were not simply arrested or set to humiliating tasks. They were killed.

A week or so later a letter arrived from Auntie Yi-feng, who lived in a village near my grandfather's house in Qingyang. As we deciphered her unpunctuated sentences and characters with bits missing, we had our worst fears confirmed. The fighting had spread strife throughout the countryside, the peasants were at war, and my paternal grandfather was right in the middle. He was attacked because he used to be a businessman and had owned a plot of land. First his house in Qingyang was confiscated and he and Grandmother were left with only one room while other families moved in. Next the rebels slaughtered his chickens, rabbits and goats to "cut off his capitalist tail," that is, deprive him of his sideline. When he tried to stop the crazed rebels from tearing down the "bourgeois" grave mounds of his mother, his first wife and my parents, he was so badly beaten that he had to be carried home on a door, and had been confined to bed ever since. Not long after, Grandfather died of his injuries.

He was cremated, against his and Grandmother's will. The rosewood coffin he had had made when he turned fifty was broken up by the rebels and sold for making furniture. Preparing one's own funeral far ahead of time was traditional, and many believed that the better provided you were, the later the funeral would occur. I had seen Great-Aunt making her tiny red silk burial shoes even before she retired, each with a ladder stitched on the sole to help her climb to heaven. The Red Guards had labelled this tradition as "belonging to the Four Olds," and punished it severely. My neighbour Granny Ningbo had been made to walk down our lane wearing all her burial outfit, followed by jeering children, then to throw the clothing into a bonfire. She died soon after the humiliation. I wondered, in Grandfather's case, how great a part humiliation had played in his death, as he was a well-known and highly respected resident of Qingyang before the rebels attacked him.

———

By the time my sixteenth birthday approached, the country's food productivity had dropped alarmingly. In the countryside, Auntie Yi-feng wrote, crops were neglected or not sown at all. "Better to have proletarian weeds than capitalist seeds," screamed the posters. Hunger began to stalk the country again.

Probably because he realized the damage caused by the chaos across China, Mao urged us to, "Grasp revolution in one hand, boost productivity with the other," and called upon young people to "resume classes while continuing to make revolution." In May, after two years of idleness, I received a letter authorized by the Mao Ze-dong Thought Propaganda Team calling me back to school.

I welcomed an end to boredom and wasted time, but I knew it was not the end of harassment from the Red Guards, so I went back with mixed feelings. Ai Guo Middle School was then in the hands of a new administration, composed of politically appointed workers, none of them qualified to run a school. Their leader required the teachers and students to address her as Master Ma. There was no sign whatever that classes would resume, as my letter had said. The teachers who had survived the cruel attacks from their own students and colleagues did not dare to teach. The students, after two years of challenging authority and humiliating their teachers, found it hard to sit down again. Most of our textbooks had been labelled "poisonous weeds," but there were no new ones to replace them.

So, despairing that I would never get enough education to try the university entrance exams, I submitted once again to the required reading of newspapers and Mao's quotations. Not long after the recall, I found out the real reason for it: we were all—the entire school population—being de-enrolled in July! There were to be no exams: they had been abolished as "bourgeois tools" used to "discriminate against working-class children by barring them from higher learning." We had to leave the school to make room for younger kids like my little sister, who had never been to middle school but would be a second-year student as soon as she walked in the door, and graduate a year later.

"I won't even have time to warm my seat in my new school," she scoffed.

So, after barely two years of proper junior middle-school education, I "graduated" at sixteen. My dream of completing senior middle school and going to university went up in smoke, for I had to join the work force. To make things even more ridiculous, while I and others were "waiting for work," we were required to report to our school every day, even though there were no classes! We sat around talking and playing cards.

I was now confronted with a harsh and unexpected reality and it frightened me. How was I going to support myself?

Since all jobs were filled according to the government's design, there was no such thing as applying for a position. A graduate of secondary school who did not go to university simply waited until the government assigned him or her a job. Those with connections "used the back door" to land favourable assignments, the most coveted of all being in the army because of its social status and security. Sick at heart, I filled out the official form, at the top of which, of course, was "political fitness," that is, class background. I also had to list all my siblings, with their ages, occupations and schools.

But what terrified me most was a new government policy, supposedly designed to relieve the pressure of overpopulation in the cities. One child from each family must move to the countryside and remain there for the rest of his or her life. Students who were the only child in their family were safe, guaranteed a job in the city, and those with siblings already working outside Shanghai had winners' smiles on their faces. But for my family, the relocation policy meant disaster.

If the government had wanted to cause conflict in families, it couldn't have picked a better method. No one born in an urban area would ever voluntarily give up his or her city residency and live in the country, for country living in China was a life of hardship and deprivation. Now, long before we expected, both Number 3 and I had become middle-school "graduates." Since Number 1 was still at university, Number 2 already had a job in Shanghai and Number 5 had just become a middle-school student, either my older sister or I would have to leave the city and live the harsh life of a peasant until she died.

How I wished time would stop. I counted every hour until October when the axe would fall on the "graduates" of my year. I reminded myself of Great-Aunt's optimistic saying that a boat carried by the river's current would always straighten itself out before it came to the bridge. But I wasn't so sure. The battles in families intensified as siblings fought like enemies. One of my classmates, who had walked out on her adoptive parents and denounced them as capitalist bloodsuckers, now realized that when she returned to her biological family, where she had siblings, she had given up her "only child" status within her adoptive family for an uncertain future. She feared she would be the one chosen to go to the countryside. She begged forgiveness from her adoptive parents, but they were brokenhearted and refused to take her back.

I had no one to share my troubles with or to advise me. Great-Aunt never liked to talk over problems; she relied on her homily about the boat. My older brothers had replaced my parents in many ways, but I didn't want to burden them. Whatever they decided between Number 3 and me would leave one of us bitter and disappointed. Some of my classmates came to school with horror stories of their parents' suffering, wracked with guilt and indecision when they had to pick one of their children to send away. I desperately missed my father's guidance, and yet I couldn't forget Mother's agony when she had to choose which of her sons would sacrifice his education to support the family.

The tension in our home grew to be unbearable. No one would discuss our dilemma. More than once I wished that a big fight would break out to clear the air. Maybe family conflict could be helpful at times. But after many years of growing closer together because of the death of our parents and our suffering in political storms, we could not face a clash.

In mid-October I was called back to the office and confronted by Master Wang, a worker from a nearby refrigeration-equipment factory who was part of the Propaganda Team. He informed me officially that it was time for me to give an answer. Would I or my elder sister be the one to leave Shanghai? I begged him to make an exception for us, saying that both I and Number 3 were needed at home to take care of our baby sister, as we had no parents.

"As far as I am concerned, all three of you should go," he shot back. "Children like you, spoiled rotten by your bourgeois parents, ought to be sent away to see the real world. Yes, that is what I am going to recommend."

His pen hovered over the official form. I stood there crying, stung by every word and terrified by this threat.

"I'll go," I stammered. "I'll leave. But please leave my two sisters in Shanghai!"

"If I agree to that, you'll go at the first opportunity?"

"Yes!"

With that one word, I sealed my fate.

CHAPTER TEN

—

I ran to Number 3's school, more than a kilometre away,
frantic to get there before she too was forced to "agree" to go
to the countryside. There I signed a paper, witnessed by
Number 3's teacher and a member of her school's Propaganda
Team, saying I was willing to be sent to the countryside.

As I walked home I felt as if a heavy burden had dropped
from my shoulders. Finally the tension that had been oppress-
ing us would be broken. Many would have thought that
Number 3 should have been the one to go because she was two
years older. Certainly that was what Great-Aunt was hoping
for, although she never said a word.

I had always felt guilty about Great-Aunt's favouritism
toward me and had occasionally hurt her feelings as a result.
I wished she would treat us all equally, or show more concern

for Number 5, who needed more care. My leaving Shanghai would hurt Great-Aunt deeply, and she would inevitably resent Number 3, but I was also aware that if I stayed and let Number 3 go, my conscience would give me no rest.

All the way home I tried to think up reasons to persuade Great-Aunt that I should be the one to leave, so she wouldn't take it out on Number 3. That evening at dinner, when I told my family my decision, I was greeted by silence and bowed heads, then Number 3 began to cry. I didn't tell them about Master Wang's threats because I thought I would look stupid. Later I talked to Great-Aunt alone in her room.

"I should have known it would be you," she sighed, using her sleeve to wipe away a tear. "Ah Si, the dragon-year girl. If your mother had let me adopt you, you would be considered an only child and you could stay here with me."

I told her that Number 3 would not be safe away from home because she was accident-prone. Hadn't she hurt herself three times in one year in her physical education class? The first time, she had chipped a front tooth; the second ended with five stitches in the chin; the third brought cerebral concussion and a trip to the hospital. How would she survive in the countryside? I argued.

As usual, reason was lost on Great-Aunt. "A clumsy person will be well taken care of," she said, "maybe even exempted from physical labour. But who will look after you, Ah Si?"

—

Master Wang wasted no time in hustling me out of Shanghai. Two weeks later at a meeting of us middle school "graduates" he gave me two options: I could go to a rubber plantation on Hainan Island in the South China Sea, a place I had heard of but knew nothing about, or to a prison farm, far north of Shanghai in Jiangsu Province.

"Probably your father the capitalist rubber manufacturer would have loved to see you working in a rubber plantation," he remarked to hoots of laughter from the other girls. "You have forty-eight hours to decide, or I'll decide for you."

Stung by anger and humiliation, what I felt most was panic. What on earth did he mean—a prison farm? As far as I knew, Shanghai graduates were always sent to farms on Chong Ming Island at the mouth of the Yangtze, a four-hour boat trip from the city. And why was I the only student in the school given forty-eight hours to come to a decision?

Our physical education instructor, Teacher Chen, took me aside and said quietly that the reason I had become the first target was because my name was at the top of the school's welfare list, so if I was sent away they could save money. She added that if I refused to comply—as some others, backed by their parents, would—my monthly allowance would be cut off immediately. Even worse, Number 3 would not be assigned a job until I left the city. Our household, always short of money, would lose two incomes.

For the first time in my sixteen years, I wished I had never been born into this world. I called the university and left an urgent message for Number 1 to come home. I needed his counsel badly. That night I told him I thought I should go to Hainan Island, my reason being that since it was tropical I would be spared the expense of winter clothing. Most of all, though, I was terrified at the thought of living with hardened criminals at the other place. While speaking to him, I lost control, where earlier I had refused to shed a single tear at school.

"Why do they want to send me to a prison farm?" I cried. "What have I done to deserve this?"

My family kept silent, not knowing what to say, and we all went to bed before dinner.

The next morning Number 1 asked me to stay at home while he tried to find out more information. My other siblings went out too, leaving me alone with Great-Aunt, who had cried quietly the whole night through. Now she bustled around, pretending to be busy. Watching her, I realized how much I was going to miss her. I wished she would tell me how much she loved me and how she didn't want me to leave her.

By lunchtime Number 1 had returned with news. He had visited the Farm Management Bureau of East China Region and talked to a clerk there. The rubber plantation, he said, was in one of the poorest areas in China and had long suffered a devastating outbreak of hepatitis. That was one of the reasons new workers were being recruited. The prison farm was called Da Feng, Big Harvest, and was near the coast of the Yellow Sea. The farm had been set up in the early 1950s to put away political prisoners; later it became a labour camp for other criminals.

"But they're all minor offenders, Ah Si," Number 1 tried to reassure me. "And some of them have been sent there because of their dissolute lifestyle. They won't harm you so long as you keep away from them."

I had learnt from *da-zi-bao* that "dissolute lifestyle" referred to men who, like my great-grandfather, had had more than one wife, or to those who messed around with others' spouses. Unmarried people caught "sleeping together" were also in this category.

I felt only a little better. It seemed that either choice would be hell on earth. Being sixteen was supposed to be like opening the first page to a bright future. To me it was as if someone had shut the book of life in my face.

I chose the prison farm.

—

One week later, Teacher Chen came to our home and brought with her the official notice of my assignment. My departure date was November 20, less than two weeks away. Only after I had left Shanghai would Number 3 be assigned a job, the notice said.

"Ah Si! I don't want you to go!" Number 5 cried.

Everyone, even Great-Aunt, began to cry except me. I kept reminding myself that tears would only make everyone feel worse. Besides, in two weeks, totally alone and cut off, I would have all the time in the world to weep.

When we had all calmed down a bit, Teacher Chen pointed out that the notice contained a number of rules and regulations. First and most important, I had to terminate my city *hu-kou*, the most vital thing I had next to life itself, so that my residence could be transferred to the prison farm. In China at that time only about 20 percent of the population had urban *hu-kou* and thus enjoyed better food and other supplies, because the city industries provided more than three-fifths of the nation's revenue, not to mention the fact that Shanghai was one of only three cities directly under the central government. Beijing and Tianjin were the others. Even my younger sister was aware that if the Shanghainese had to tighten their belts, farmers were starving. Once I lost my *hu-kou* I could never get it back again. It was the symbol of exile.

Second, the winter was cold there, the notice said. There was no indoor heating system. Bring warm clothes and extra bedding.

Early next morning I left home, glad to escape the funereal silence. I turned in my *hu-kou* and ration coupons at the local police station and was issued food coupons valid anywhere in the country along with special certificates for a pair of rubber shoes, one cotton-blend blanket, and a mosquito net, and for raw cotton and fabric to make clothes and bedding.

When I got home, Number 2 was waiting for me. We sat down at the dinner table and he handed me one hundred yuan, a king's ransom, more money than any of us had ever seen in our lives.

"I borrowed it from my factory," he said, "so you can buy anything you need or want."

I was moved to tears. It would take him years to pay back such a huge sum. I didn't know how to thank him. And at the same time, staring at the money through tear-filled eyes, I realized with an awful finality that I was going away from my family, from the apartment where I was born and raised, for the rest of my life.

"Don't cry, Ah Si," he said. "Everything will be all right. Come on, Number 1 is waiting to take you to the stores."

Throughout the shopping trip with my eldest brother I hardly paid attention as he led me through crowded stores and purchased cotton ticking and cloth to make winter clothing. But as we passed one store window what caught my eye, of all things, was a pair of colourful nylon socks, smooth and stretchy and looking like they would fit comfortably. After years of wearing socks mended so often that I had to wear shoes at least a size too large, they seemed to me the height of luxury. I asked Number 1 to buy me a pair. He bought me two.

Mother used to say that "far away relatives are not as dear as close neighbours," and she was absolutely right, for our neighbours pitched in to help me prepare for my exile. Mrs. Yan was burning the midnight oil making my padded coat and pants.

"The farm is called Da Feng, isn't it?" she said. "It must be bloody cold there!" She thought Da Feng meant Big Wind because *feng*, meaning wind, sounds the same as *feng*, for harvest.

Ying-ying's mother's support was also practical. She gave me two rolls of high-quality toilet paper, white as snow and soft as cotton, which she had bought in the special Overseas Chinese store before the Cultural Revolution. She told me that when I had my period, if I had to walk a lot I should wrap this tissue around the rough sanitary paper.

Great-Aunt kept herself busy all the time, so busy she said she didn't have time to talk to me. That was typical. Whenever she was sad or angry, silence was her response. She sat in front of the coal stove hour after hour, day after day, roasting flour in a wok, stirring it carefully so it wouldn't burn. Roast flour was cheap and handy, and when mixed with boiled water it swelled up and filled the stomach. If a little sugar was added, it became a treat. But the procedure took tremendous time and patience and I was shocked to see how much Great-Aunt had prepared for me. She had used up all her food coupons, plus some she had borrowed from neighbours, to buy the flour. That too was typical.

In the following days and at nights as we lay side by side, I waited for Great-Aunt to tell me to watch out for myself because I would be alone, and that she would miss me. I yearned for her to say that somehow we would make do without my welfare stipend or a job for Number 3 and that I wouldn't have to leave home after all.

By that point in my life, I should have known that hope itself was a fantasy.

PART TWO

—

DA FENG PRISON FARM

CHAPTER ELEVEN

—

After an overnight passage on the ship, *The East Is Red, Number 8*, a flaking hulk crammed with miserable teenagers, I climbed aboard a decrepit bus to begin the long ride north of the Yangtze River to the prison farm. The fields around the city of Nangtong in Jiangsu Province soon fell away behind our convoy and we entered a flat and not quite believable landscape, swept by wind so strong it forced its way around the edges of the windows into the buses. For kilometre after kilometre there was not a tree, a building or a human being to be seen under the grey November sky. Raised in one of the country's largest cities, I had never seen a street empty of people, not even in the middle of the night. I was no expert in country living, but in the countryside surrounding Qingyang, where, before Father's operation, we had travelled every year to visit Grandfather, I had always seen farmers working in fields divided by narrow paddy dikes, or walking the dirt roads. There, even in winter, the densely populated land was green and the air heavy with humidity and the rich odours of growing plants. This emptiness could mean only one thing: the soil was no good for farming.

"House, house!" someone yelled from the front of the bus. We had been rattling along for five hours. Through the dust-coated window I saw a cluster of thatch-roofed buildings. The bus turned off the road and bumped through a village on a rutted track. It turned onto a wider road blanketed with white powder. The unfamiliar substance also covered the fields, and seemed like a permanent feature.

The buses ahead of us began to peel off onto narrow dirt roads to the left and right. Mine rumbled across a wooden bridge and pulled up in the midst of a cluster of wattle build-ings thatched with rice straw. Everyone fell silent, staring. Around the buildings, desolation: flat, dry, empty fields. I told myself that this must be just a temporary stop.

When the door flapped open, letting in the chilly wind, a middle-aged man stepped up into the bus. "Hello, revolution-ary comrades!" he greeted us in a Su Bei accent, using a term that had been out of date since the beginning of the Cultural Revolution. "Welcome to the Number One Brigade of Xia Ming Sub-farm of Da Feng Labour Camp . . . er, Da Feng Farm," he corrected himself hastily. "Xia Ming is one of five sub-farms; each has six brigades. My name is Chang Wen, and I am the leader of this brigade."

Reluctantly I stepped down from the bus with the others. The welcoming team consisted of Lao Chang's assistant, Lao Deng—a short old man whose mouth and eye-corners pointed up, even when he wasn't smiling; their wives; the doctor; and the accountant. The latter, a tall skinny man, shook hands with each of us, bowing deeply as he did so and smiling, showing his cigarette–stained teeth. Shaking hands was a novel experience for me, as it suggested I was now an adult.

I looked around, searching for some sign of scar-faced criminals, high walls or stout buildings with barred windows, but saw nothing out of the ordinary, just a tiny village with dirt roads and pathways. Dr. Wang, the youngest of the greeting party, whose sharp, bright eyes reminded me of my grandfather, asked the male students to follow him to their dormitory. Lao Bai, Lao Chang's wife, a chubby middle-aged woman with a piercing voice, called for the females.

"Is this where we're going to stay?" someone shouted from the men's dorm.

Our dorm was, like all the buildings, single-story, made of wattle—woven sticks and straw plastered with clay and mud—with a thatched roof and dirt floor. It was on the south side of the village, separated from the men's dorm by a pathway and from the empty fields by a ditch.

"Come on," Lao Bai said. "Pay no attention to him. Come in and have a look."

We filed through the narrow door. My first impression was of heavy odours of dampness, lime, smoke and rotten rice straw. The building was like an oversized train coach, about fifteen metres long but only six wide. Though it was mid-afternoon, three naked bulbs fought to dispel the gloom. There was a door at each end and three small windows on each side. The dirt floor had been packed hard by many feet; the walls were newly whitewashed, but brown clay was already oozing through. Along each wall ran a low platform of undressed boards supported by sharpened tree branches driven into the dirt and covered with malodorous straw. This was our bed.

As if she had seen into my mind, Lao Bai said cheerfully, "It won't look so bad when you've all spread out your bedding. You city girls are good at decorating, aren't you? Soon this place will look like home."

After a short but determined tussle during which many angled to be with their schoolmates or near the windows and everybody fought to stay away from the doors, territory was marked out by the small canvas shoulder bags we all carried. Lao Bai then led us to the canteen on the north edge of the village for a late lunch. Before entering, I looked around for a tap to wash my hands. I spied half a dozen water jars outside a small building, each one as high as my chest and as wide as my outstretched arms. Every one of them was filled with clean water, though it smelled of mud. This shack must be a pump house, I thought, and wondered how I could wash my hands without contaminating the whole jar.

A white-haired man appeared from behind a hut, where he had evidently been working, for his hands were black.

"Can I help you, young miss?"

I explained my predicament.

"Come with me," he said quietly, and led me through the door of the shack. On the floor was a basin with soap and a towel beside it. He motioned me to use them, then left me alone. Outside again, I scooped a basin full of water from one of the jars, thinking that this must be the village's fresh water supply.

Once inside the canteen I was asked by several students how I had managed to wash, since none of our luggage had arrived. I told them, adding that the basin, towel and soap could be used by them too, for the old uncle seemed kind enough.

"Young lady, be careful of what you are saying," Lao Bai cut in, scowling. "You should call no one here uncle or aunt, nor go to their places and use their things. Only those who greeted you on the bus today should be addressed. You must have no contact with anyone else." She lowered her voice dramatically. "You wouldn't want to be anywhere near that 'old uncle' if you knew what he had done before Liberation."

Her words sent a bolt of fear through me. Had I been speaking to one of the criminals? Was he a murderer?

"You, all of you," Lao Bai went on, "stay away from them. You are all young girls. You never know what those curs are up to. If you have to, just call them *Wei*, nothing else."

Wei means "Hey, you!" in Chinese, or "Hello" while talking on the telephone. We had been taught all our lives to call a man Uncle or Old Uncle, depending on his age; a woman was Auntie or Old Auntie. To address anyone older than you, even a stranger, by saying only "Wei" was disrespectful.

Lao Bai's warning had destroyed my appetite. I repeatedly stole glances at the men standing behind the counter, the ones who had served up our food. No wonder they stood there like blocks of wood, expressionless. No wonder they had said nothing to us and avoided eye contact. But if they were as dangerous and untrustworthy as Lao Bai said, why should we trust the food they prepared?

At a meeting that evening Lao Chang cautioned us never to use the public toilet at night. He didn't specify whether he was afraid we would be molested by prisoners or fall into the open manure pit beside the unlit latrine. His warning didn't help my attempts to fall asleep. Around me the other girls talked, sobbed or cried out in their sleep. I was utterly discouraged. I felt as if we were all little lambs in the jungle, waiting to be slaughtered.

When I awoke I found myself encroaching on my bed-neighbour's space. It would take us a while, I thought, to get used to sleeping together on the long bench. Her name was Liu Lanlan—Orchid—a senior-high graduate of Xiang Yang middle school in the same district as my school. From her puffed eyes I gathered that her night's sleep had been no better than mine. As soon as we were out of bed she began to clean and tidy her spot, her long thin body a bundle of nervous energy as she tried in vain to arrange her sheet neatly on the straw.

My neighbour to my right turned out to be one of my schoolmates, although I didn't know her well. Jia-ying was a pretty nineteen-year-old with big dark eyes and a pale oval face, her hair trimmed stylishly. When she introduced me to my other three schoolmates in her soft voice, she sounded like an organizer at a social event. In fact, organization was not her strong suit: there were unwashed bowls under her bed, jumbled clothing piled on her open luggage. A little later she asked shyly if I would hold up a sheet so that she could huddle behind it to change her clothes.

Standing on her bed with the sheet in my hands, I had a good view of the long narrow dorm, filled with young women—all of them at least two years older than me—walking to and fro in their underwear while others squatted on the spittoons that were used for chamber pots, a scene I knew would be repeated endlessly in the weeks, months and years to come.

The opening of the day was a parade to the latrine, with many carrying their chamber pots amid giggles and sarcastic remarks from the male students and the prisoners. When I saw the women's latrine I repeated to myself the overpraised expression "Everything is hard at the beginning," but suspected that in this case the difficulty would never diminish. Reed mats formed the walls. The thatched roof was obviously not waterproof. The dirt floor was slotted by a series of ditches, over which we would squat, one foot on each side. An inside wall, no more than three metres high, separated our latrine from the men's, from which laughter and the smell of cigarettes came clearly.

I had grown up in an environment in which emphasizing personal needs was criticized as bourgeois garbage; nevertheless, I had always tried to keep personal matters to myself.[13] Although this was not my first experience of relieving myself

---

13. "Bourgeois" was a critical term meaning "opposed to Party policies" or "anti-revolutionary."

in such an open and exposed way—the Beijing trip had given me a startling awakening—I found it hard to cope. I walked gingerly to a corner ditch, farthest from the men's side, amazed at how casual some of the women were, chatting to one another from a squatting position, calling out to new arrivals, saying goodbye to those departing.

Before breakfast I stole off by myself and inspected the village. It didn't take long. The camp was made up of four rows of buildings: the first two were residences and dorms, the rest, on the north side of the central road, housed the clinic, administration offices, canteens and pump houses, and the warehouse for storing tools and farm equipment. The perimeter on three sides was a wide ditch, partly filled with sluggish water and littered with garbage, which connected to a river on the fourth side. It was a desolate and featureless place.

I got to the canteen just in time to hear Lao Chang's first lecture, arms behind his back, to the new arrivals. He had stuffed himself into a faded army uniform, complete with a cap, and made every effort to sound official and important. My eyes were drawn to the strained stitches on his shoulders and the five buttons of his jacket, which were making a valiant effort to hold the coat together.

Lao Chang was a "Thirty-eighter," one of those who had joined the Communist Party in 1938 and taken part in the war against the Japanese invaders. Being a Thirty-eighter meant high status and prestige. There were other honourifics, such as Long Marcher (one who endured the famous 12,500-kilometre trek with Mao Ze-dong in 1934); White Area

Underground Activist (a Communist undercover agent in a Guomindang-controlled area), and Soviet-area Worker (one who worked in the Communist bases established during the Second Revolutionary Civil War against the Guomindang from 1927 to 1937). In my understanding, these designations were like expensive liquor: the earlier bottled, the better.

Lao Chang opened his speech with good news. Each of us would earn eighteen yuan per month—double my welfare allowance. I was ecstatic. Finally, after nearly a lifetime of poverty and humiliation as a welfare recipient, I would be supporting myself, earning a real wage! I would be able to send money to help my family.

Next, with his hands still clasped behind him, rocking as he spoke, Lao Chang told us about the prisoners. There were eighty-seven of them in the brigade, all males, all from Shanghai.

"Where are the female prisoners?" one young woman interrupted.

"Does that mean they can go back home to Shanghai when they have served their time?" a young man asked. "Why can't we go home, then?"

Lao Chang made no attempt to hide his annoyance at having his speech pushed off the rails. "All the female prisoners are at the Chuan Dong Sub-farm," he said sternly. "So far as I am concerned, mixing males and females spells one word: trouble."

Years later I learned that Lao Chang's bitterness about women came from experience. He had been punished for having an affair with a married woman in his work unit and banished to the farm for his "rotten lifestyle." His wife and family had accompanied him, and his "assignment" was indefinite.

"As for you, young man," he continued, "I will not reply to your ill-mannered interruption." His voice became shrill. "When I was your age I was laying my life on the line for our motherland so that you could live the easy life you have now. Don't take your own good fortune for granted."

He then stood aside for Lao Deng, who informed us in his quavering voice that this farm had been reclaimed from the Yellow Sea, and that every winter there was a massive labour campaign to repair and strengthen the dikes along the seashore. The farm's soil, he went on to say, was so alkaline that, after a summer shower the heat would form salt rocks around the village. As a matter of fact, the closest town, about forty-five kilometres to the northwest, was called Yan Cheng—Salt City. Because of the quality of the soil, the main crops of the area had been cotton and peanuts, along with some vegetables. Since the inception of the National Program for Agricultural Development, great efforts had been made in the last few years to grow rice, but without much success. Nevertheless, he said ominously, these efforts would continue.

Most of his words went in one ear and out the other. I was a city girl. Surely one crop was the same as another. Soon I would learn the hard way how wrong I was.

Lao Deng finally left off speaking and we lined up to get our breakfast. Afterwards we had to run a gauntlet of prisoners who had been standing outside the canteen waiting for their turn. Most were shabbily dressed, their coats held closed by the braided rice-straw belts. All wore padded hats with earflaps. They banged their enamel bowls and yelled and laughed at us, making rude remarks to some of the female students.

"First you steal our house and now our food!" one of them hollered above the racket.

Apparently the dorms we had moved into the night before had been theirs and they had been forced to live in even less-inviting quarters. I didn't blame them for their anger; but they still frightened me as I hurried past holding my two bowls.

That first day I and my new farm-mates, who were almost all "non-red" students, began our field labour. It soon became evident that Mrs. Yan's mistake about the name of the farm—calling it Big Wind instead of Big Harvest—was grimly appropriate, for all day and night an icy-cold wind swept out of the northwest. A local rhyme described it: on odd days the wind rolled up the land like a rug; on even days it unrolled it again. Although the water in the river and the jars outside the pump house seldom froze, our proximity to the sea ensured that the almost-freezing air was heavy and damp.

The first thing I learned was to pick cotton—not to harvest the puffy white balls, for the prisoners had picked them more than a month before, in October, but rather to go from bush to bush and strip the unripened pods from the bare branches. The pods had to be torn open by hand so that the sticky black substance inside could be collected and later shipped to a mill to be pressed for cooking oil. Before long my hands were raw and red from cold and the abrasive pods. When that job was complete, we had to pull the cotton plants from the ground, a backbreaking task. Lao Deng was determined that rice would be planted there the next season.

One night several weeks after we had begun working in the fields, I found Jia-ying weeping silently in bed.

"What's wrong?" I asked.

She showed me her swollen fingers, her raw and scratched skin. "How can I ever play the piano again with hands like these?"

I picked up my pillow cover, a small towel, and wrapped it around her hands. "They will heal, Jia-ying. Don't worry. Our work in the cotton fields will be over soon."

"Over?" she scoffed. "It will never be over." She threw the towel at me and crawled under her quilt.

Even though I believed in the healing of wounds, I doubted that our invisible wounds would ever be remedied.

Our long days in the cold, desolate fields did not earn us any free time. Between dinner and lights-out we had political study in the dorm. Usually one of the two Laos would join us to lead the obligatory readings and discussions of government policies and campaigns as we sat on the end of our trestle bed and went through the motions. Tired and aching all over, I would try in vain to find a comfortable position. On those occasions when the Laos failed to appear, the study session was run by our team leader. We would climb into bed and wrap ourselves in our cotton-ticked quilts and soon our discussions would go off topic. At these times, driven by cold and boredom, I was prone to make jokes and kid around.

My sense of humour was honed by hardship. I always seemed keenly aware of ironies, and the Cultural Revolution provided an endless supply. The hated little red book, linked in my mind to suffering, nevertheless reminded me of the world I knew back home. Yet, even while the thought of spending my life on the farm plunged me into depression, letters from home made me realize how peaceful it was here, a forgotten corner in a crazy world, free of the strife, the endless campaigns, the fighting in factory and street.

And so, in silence and loneliness, the new year arrived.

CHAPTER TWELVE

—

To celebrate the New Year, Lao Chang ordered the cooks to slaughter a pig, which put broad smiles on our faces. For many weeks we had had nothing to eat with our rice but preserved vegetables and dried fish so loaded with salt that it reminded me of stories of the Red Army, half-starved on the Long March, having to lick salt blocks for strength.

All of us arrived at the canteen half an hour early. As I waited in line with the others, anticipating the savoury odour and rich taste of pork, I recalled the many times when Mrs. Yan would wake me up at four in the morning so we could go to the market to queue up for a piece of pork fat. The fat required fewer coupons than meat, and Great-Aunt found it valuable as a flavouring for freshly cooked rice, with a bit of salt or soybean sauce. My hunger also reminded me of the day a few weeks before when I discovered Jia-ying had brought a can of chicken fat from home and I tried not to show my jealousy.

When our meal began, I chewed my one thin piece of pork, cooked in soybean sauce and edged with fat and skin, as slowly as possible, relishing every bite. It was heavenly.

After dinner, while I was rinsing my dishes at the pump station with Jia-ying, several gaunt and bedraggled prisoners began to yell at us. For the first time at New Year they had been denied meat; instead, they had been fed bones, intestines and nameless organs.

"You useless city brats have ripped the food from our mouths," they snarled. We ran off with our dirty dishes, followed by their curses.

Two days later they got their revenge. Although we had been repeatedly warned not to move around on our own, not even during the day, I insisted on going to the latrine by myself, for I had my period and did not want to change my napkins with others around. Everyone else had gone to the rice-threshing ground to fetch new straw for our beds. I was gratified to find the latrine empty.

A few moments later I heard rustling. Thinking there must be a bat in the thatched roof—a fairly common occurrence— I covered my ears, for I had been told that bats like to crawl into people's heads. At the same time I closed my eyes and bent my head between my knees, hoping no one would come in and see me in such a ridiculous position, pants around my ankles, squatting over the trench.

"How are you, my dear?"

Startled, I opened my eyes and saw a man's hand waving at me over the top of the partition.

"Why don't you come over here, young lady? From what I can see, we'll be friends in no time."

I opened my mouth to scream but no sound came out. I jumped up, pulled up my pants, and ran all the way to the dorm, which was, luckily, unlocked that day because two girls were in bed with the flu.

Shaking with fear, I told them what had happened. Later, I wished I had never opened my mouth. An investigation started. I was interviewed twice by Lao Chang and each time I had to repeat my embarrassing tale. I was questioned by the two wives, the doctor and the accountant. When they returned from their work, my dorm-mates badgered me for details. Soon everyone, even the men, knew about the incident, including the fact that I had made a mess on my clothes in my hasty exit. Why is it, I wondered, that *I* should be the one made to feel like a fool?

—

My relatively peaceful but lonely life was disturbed one bitterly cold day in mid-January when I got a letter from Number 2. Number 3 had finally been assigned a job, he wrote, but not in Shanghai. She had been sent to a factory in Songjiang County that made small electronic meter parts. It was near the commune where I had spent two weeks working with the peasants before the Cultural Revolution began. Despite my sacrifice in volunteering to go to the countryside so that my elder sister could remain in Shanghai and look after our little sister, Number 3 had had to move outside the city anyway, and could go home only on weekends.

"Number 3 did not protest," my brother wrote. "She knew it would be pointless."

And it was a good thing she didn't, he went on. Just one week after Number 3's assignment, in late December, Mao Ze-dong issued a new call, ordering *all* city middle-school graduates to the countryside, including kids from "red" families, who had been exempt when I was "sent down." Mao described rural work assignments as "a vast world where much can be accomplished; a boundless field for youngsters to use their talents." If Number 3 hadn't accepted the job, she too would have been sent to the countryside.

"The whole city," wrote Number 2, "is like a funeral home for the living. Instead of catching fish one by one, as in your case, Ah Si, Mao has cast a wider net."

Obviously, letters received by others spread the same news, for the result was vengeful laughter and grim satisfaction. Usually the arrival of the mail brought tears of homesickness, but not this time. All of us had been banished to this remote farm rather than to the much more civilized farms on Chong Ming Island because of our "bad class background"; now those who had harassed and humiliated us at school and on the streets would suffer the same fate. Lan-lan told me that two of her classmates who had shaved her mother's head during a

Red Guard raid on their house were being sent to Heilongjiang Province, far to the north, near the Russian border, a place where, according to legend, black bears would knock at your door and your breath turned to icicles.

"It serves them right!" she said bitterly. "I hope their noses and ears turn to ice and fall off!"

The next morning at a mass meeting in the warehouse Lao Chang briefed us on some new government documents. Lao Chang, I had noticed, loved these gatherings because in his eyes his prestige among his colleagues and their families, as well as the prisoners, was enhanced when he was addressing more than sixty middle-school graduates. He had held meetings on everything from the importance of cotton plants to making straw mattresses and ropes.

In order to respond to Chairman Mao's call to make rice the key crop and to ensure year-round planting to build China's self-reliance, we would be converting most of the cotton fields to rice paddies, he announced pompously. This was hardly news. We had been yanking the cotton plants out of the unyielding ground for ages and most of us had the bandaged hands to prove it. Our accountant, Lao Shi, stood up and assured us that as long as we could harvest rice once a year we would have a surplus, and he shook his abacus to confirm his calculations. With the others, I applauded this announcement, thinking that any crop must be easier than cotton.

"More city kids are coming!" Lao Chang crowed excitedly when he regained the floor. "We must build new houses for them. They'll be here in four weeks."

All the male labourers, including the prisoners, were to go to the dike to cut reeds and haul them back to the village on wagons drawn by water buffalo. We females would make bundles of reeds for walls and roofs.

I was less enthusiastic than Lao Chang about the arrival of more students. They would be politically correct "reds," not like us, and that meant only one thing—conflict and persecution, attacks and humiliation, with people like me on the receiving end.

CHAPTER THIRTEEN

—

In March, fifty-six wide-eyed youths stepped down from the decrepit buses to the beating of gongs and drums. They did not seem as cowed as we had been when we first set foot on the alkaline soil of the prison farm.

Awaiting them were two brand-new dorms, still smelling of fresh reeds and the lime coating on the inner walls. We had hoped we might move into the new dorms ourselves: the early spring rains and subsequent dampness had covered our walls with green mould. So many evenings I had awakened to damp bedding and the *plink-plunk* of rain dropping through the roof into the rice bowls and washbasins we had scattered around. More often, I was startled by sudden screams when someone discovered unrecognized creatures crawling inside their bedding. But Lao Chang said no; we were "veterans" now and should yield the new dorms to the novices.

These fresh arrivals were not the scared and compliant beings we had been—and still were. Within a week Lao Chang was confronted by a newly formed committee of students and informed that he was no longer in charge of the welfare of the school youngsters. His connection to us from that day on was only as a production consultant. The self-appointed committee consisted of two women and three men. At the first meeting, each stood up and claimed to be *san-dai-hong*—three generations red—working-class as far back as their grandfathers. Their leadership of the brigade was thus legitimized and changes began immediately, from the reappointment of canteen staff to the reorganization of our living arrangements. Half of my original dorm-mates were replaced by red students, so as to "break up the stiff soil by mixing it with sand." It seemed that the reform of those with bad class backgrounds was to continue.

Each regrouped dorm was to be called a platoon, comprised of three squads. My squad leader, Yu Hua, a pretty young eighteen-year-old, was, of course, one of the newcomers. She told us proudly that one of her sisters was a veteran in the air force in Guangzhou Province. Since Liberation, joining the PLA had brought high status. The armed forces were even more prestigious now. For those who had political connections and didn't want their children to go to the countryside, joining the PLA had been the only way out. The "glory and honour" part was propaganda to justify the end-run around Mao's call.

From the time they put on their uniforms, these people looked forward to the day three years later when they would be demobilized and return home with the promise of a lifetime career and a high salary.

The new committee had plans for numerous meetings, political study and the assignment of self-reports and self-criticism.[14] Immediately, the committee's program met its first obstacle: physical exhaustion.

Converting cotton fields to rice paddies was a tremendous undertaking and the process was slow and laborious. First, the land was divided into paddies by building low dikes to hold the water that would be pumped in. Each paddy was then flushed two or three times to wash away as much of the alkaline salt as possible. The next stage was to enrich the soil by ploughing vegetation and composted night soil into it. The vegetation consisted of grass and any other green plants that could be found in the vicinity, cut down and carried by shoulder-pole to the paddies. The first problem was that, even though the lunar calendar said spring had arrived, it was anything but spring on our farm and there wasn't much new vegetation around yet. "The cleverest housewife cannot make a meal without rice," the old saying puts it, but the red students claimed that man could and would conquer nature.

---

14. In a self-criticism you were required to examine your actions and thoughts and to report, verbally and in writing, your "errors"—anything you thought or did that was not approved by the Party. Saying you had done nothing wrong only aroused more suspicion.

For weeks, each morning saw us leaving the village with shoulder-poles and straw-rope net bags, searching for anything green except reeds, for they would not decompose quickly enough. Each of us had a daily quota, which rose as the weather warmed. No matter how hard I worked, yanking and ripping weeds, grass and even some leaves with my bare hands, I couldn't get my name off the "failure" list posted in the canteen every day, accompanied by a red minus sign.

One night when I was washing my blistered feet and complaining worriedly to Jia-ying about my predicament, she laughed. "Isn't it about time you grew up and understood this world better, Xiao Ye? Do you really think we are working harder than you? The answer is no, but we know how to play with the rules."

Her common sense and humour reminded me of Number 3, and I felt the pang of loss that visited me every day, sometimes when I least expected it. I missed my family and Purple Sunshine Lane, the sounds of neighbours calling their kids home, and the aromas of their cooking.

"We not only bring back the green stuff," Jia-ying went on, "but dirt besides." She smiled sweetly, showing her dimples. "If the dirt is good for growing grass, it must be good for rice too!"

From that day on I met my quota.

But I overdid it. Typical, Great-Aunt would have said. I not only made sure the vegetation I harvested had clumps of dirt on the roots, I soaked the load with water. The mushy bottoms were glued to the ground and I could hardly lift the mess up.

One day at the end of April we were called back from the fields and ordered to gather around the loudspeaker mounted on a pole in the central road. In my utter physical exhaustion and mental dullness I welcomed the command and sprawled on the dirt with the others to listen to the radio broadcast. At the Ninth Party Congress under way in Beijing, the "biggest political event in everyone's life," as the announcer intoned, there were more than fifteen hundred delegates, "elected" by ordinary citizens. Not for thirteen years had a congress like this been held. Sitting there, my shoulders and back aching, my skinny thigh muscles burning from the weight of my burden, I couldn't have cared less.

As the congress wore on I was spared the increasingly futile search for greens and the strain of toting them back, because listening to speeches over the loudspeaker was thought to be more important than tending our crops. At night I listened to committee members read documents and news bulletins, participated (on orders) in discussions, made personal "statements of belief."

The report on Lin Biao's speech opened my wounds. Any hope I had harboured that the Cultural Revolution might begin to wind down was smashed by his testimony that "its merits are the greatest while its losses are the smallest." His words forecast more political commotion, more violence and misery. The Congress "accepted" Mao's recommendation— they had to; he was the leader—and appointed Lin Biao as his successor. This fact further enhanced the PLA's status in the Cultural Revolution and laid the foundation for the army to take over almost all key structures across the country—the police, the courts, institutions of higher learning, even the jails and prison farms.

The list of newly elected members of the Central Committee was shocking because of those names not mentioned, including President Liu Shao-qi. But among those elected was Mao's fourth wife, Jiang Qing.

To everyone's surprise we were organized for a celebration on the closing day of the Congress. Trucks rolled into the compound before supper, bringing red cloth banners, paper flags and boxes of firecrackers of all sizes. In spite of myself I found the diversion exciting. We marched four abreast to the sub-farm nearly eight kilometres away under a starless April sky, guided by diesel-fuel torches. It was the most enjoyable night I had passed since my arrival at the farm.

When the shouting of slogans and singing of propaganda songs died down we filled the darkness with talking and laughing, shrieking delightedly with the detonation of every firecracker. Great-Aunt had once told me that firecrackers were traditionally used to drive devils away. For centuries they had been a part of New Year's celebrations. That night, with every cracker that exploded in the sky, I wished hard for good luck.

The next morning the figurative worship of Mao Ze-dong became literal. Each dorm was issued two plaster statues, along with pieces of red cloth and yellow paper hearts with the character *zhong*—loyalty—embossed on them, the same word Number 2 had cleverly selected as his new name. We were ordered to set up a *zhong-zhi-tai*—loyalty shrine—at each doorway. Every morning after that we stood before the shrine and held our little red books to our hearts, requesting instruction and greeting Chairman Mao with rehearsed shouts, wishing him life "forever and ever" and his successor Lin Biao, "our beloved vice-chairman, good health, always, always." We could not even fully dress or wash ourselves first, because, we were told, the adoration exercise was the first and most important political matter in our daily life.

As I stood there on the dirt floor or on my unmade bed, surrounded by waving arms, my thoughts went back to my childhood when my siblings and I accompanied Grandfather to our ancestral hall in Qingyang. Never in my life had I seen or heard of people erecting a shrine for someone still alive. Even I knew that worshipping the living guaranteed bad luck. Less than half an hour later we repeated the same words in the canteen while we waited in line for breakfast.

One day the female students were ordered to the rice-threshing ground and taught the "loyalty dance" by professionals sent out by the Shanghai city government. While we struggled to learn the steps, we sang, "Our beloved Chairman Mao, you are the sun which will never set and we are sunflowers always swirling around you . . ." Our dancing won us the title "Flowers on the Cow Shit" among the prisoners, who had watched us dancing during a work-break from spreading cow dung to dry before it was hauled to the paddies.

My genuine effort to meet my daily vegetation quota touched my squad leader, Yu Hua, who offered to pair up with me to help me out. At that time I was only about four-foot-three and weighed no more than eighty pounds, and I needed all the help I could get. Yu Hua was a strong, sturdy woman of eighteen, with short hair and a no-nonsense manner. Her kindness moved me deeply. It was the beginning of the first real friendship of my life.

We worked together well. I was quick with my sickle; she toted cuttings to the weigh station. We met our quota regularly. But the newly formed paddies were hungry monsters, eating up everything we cut. The vegetation near the farm had long since been stripped away and we had to go farther and farther afield.

One day Yu Hua and I packed a lunch of steamed buns and pickled vegetables and left right after breakfast to search for vegetation. Our shoulder-poles bounced with each step as we headed north along the main road, gathering weeds and grass as we went. After a few hours' work we spied a swampy pit in which new shoots had sprung up where the reeds had been cut. We made our way over the spongy ground to relieve ourselves. A moment later Yu Hua called out to me. She had come upon a pathway leading over a bank into a stand of plane trees. I followed her, curious to see where the path led.

Yu Hua stopped. "Look, Xiao Ye!"

I couldn't believe my eyes. Among the trees, newly in leaf, tall grass grew, uncut and undisturbed.

"We will be able to meet our quota for weeks," I said, "if we keep this secret."

We fell to work immediately and by noon two of our mesh bags were stuffed full. After our lunch break, Yu Hua shuffled off under the weight of her shoulder-pole, leaving me busy with my sickle.

After months of living day and night in a crowd of students and amongst the circus of Mao worship and dancing, I found myself alone. I worked steadily, enjoying the solitude. The breeze stirred the grass and whispered in the branches of the surrounding trees. After a while I sat down to rest, leaning against a tree, and closed my eyes. Strangely, the isolation began to make me uneasy. Why had Yu Hua been gone so long? I decided it would be better to get back to work than to think of bad things that could happen to a girl left alone. Gathering my cuttings into piles, I bent to pick up a bundle of grass and found myself staring into the empty eye sockets of a human skull.

I screamed and dropped my burden. Stumbling down the embankment into the reeds, running and falling over the soggy ground, feet and arms torn by the brittle reed stubble, I finally gained the road. Blood ran down my legs and arms. Heart pounding, chest heaving, I ran toward the village.

When I met Yu Hua I burst into tears, breathlessly describing the horror of the skull. Only after she had calmed me down did I realize that I had left my sickle and shoulder-pole behind and would not be able to meet the day's quota.

"Never mind that for now," Yu Hua said, examining the slashes on my arms and legs. "You need a doctor."

The doctor dressed my wounds, tut-tutting and wondering under his breath how such a slight young woman could have done such damage to herself. Then Lao Deng came into the clinic with Yu Hua. I braced myself for criticism for losing my tools and for the usual remarks that we spoiled bourgeois youngsters were lazy and incapable of hard work.

"Now, Xiao Ye," he began. "Let's hear your report."

When I told him where Yu Hua and I had been cutting grass and what I had seen, his reaction surprised and confused me. He seemed amused.

"You two are quite the detectives, aren't you?" he said. Then, suddenly serious, he demanded, "How did you find that grave-yard? What—"

"Graveyard?" I interrupted him. "Is that what I found? Why is it unmarked, and where are the burial mounds? The skull was just lying on the ground."

"Listen, girl, that's Wu Mao Yu—Number Five Unmarked Burial Ground, an execution site. You'd better keep your discovery and all your questions to yourself. That's an order. And don't ever go back there again!"

For the first time since I had come to Da Feng Prison Farm, I eagerly embraced a command.

Before Lao Deng left, he wrote out a chit for a new sickle and shoulder-pole and sent me away.

CHAPTER FOURTEEN

—

From the time I arrived on the farm I was aware of the prisoners' resentment of us "spoiled" city kids. We lived in dorms meant for them, they claimed bitterly, and we took rice from their mouths while they ate substandard food. Sometimes there were shortages of food and cooking oil which caused fights with their canteen staff. And it was true that there was a double standard in work assignments. While we foraged for vegetation, the prisoners had the more difficult task of tilling the paddies with plows drawn behind water buffalo. They also constructed the rice seedbeds, a laborious and exacting job, since the mud had to be smoothed by hand before the seeds were sown.

With the coming of the busy season at the beginning of June, when the emerald seedlings were ready to be transplanted to the flooded paddies, a compromise was reached under which we students had to work the same hours, with the same quotas, as the prisoners. If we didn't succeed, Lao Chang warned us, there would be ugly consequences.

Each day, when dawn broke, we were whistled awake and, after our Mao worship, we gulped down our breakfast and headed to the fields. We carefully pulled the rice shoots from the seedbeds, shook them to free the roots of soil, bundled them in straw, and carried them to the paddies, on each of which a grid had been laid out with straw ropes pegged into the dikes. Wading up to our knees between the parallel ropes, we transplanted the seedlings. It was an arduous, precise job, six seedlings across making a straight column, about four inches separating the rows. Such precision, Lao Chang instructed us, made for the most efficient weeding and harvesting. He waved a ruler, warning us that any deviation from the measurements would lead to punishment.

Our daily quota was seven twenty-five-metre columns a day. It was a backbreaking job, bending down constantly, even for someone like me, so small, the others said, that I didn't have a waist. The only relief came with the short walk from the seedbeds to the paddy and back. By the time the day ended, I could hardly straighten my back. Before long I had worn my elbows raw from resting them on my knees as I worked. My hands swelled and developed cysts from pulling out the seedlings and plunging them into the cold water. Leeches were a frightening menace. They crawled up and hung on to my legs, and I had to slap the skin hard to make them let go. Thin streams of blood flowed from the wounds. The disgusting creatures startled me so much that I often fell back onto my bottom in the cold, muddy water.

Lao Chang said timing was the key to growing rice and no delay could be tolerated. Swollen hands and feet met with no sympathy. He even went so far as to have his wife check the girls who claimed to have their periods, because, according to the rules, they were allowed two days of dry land work at such times. For the first time in my life I welcomed my period, wishing it would come weekly rather than once a month.

I lost count of the times I slept in my clothes after returning from the fields, too exhausted to clean up first, my mud-covered calves poking out from under the mosquito net. Yu Hua continued to look out for me, particularly after I told her I had no parents. "I will be your *Jie-Jie*—elder sister," she said. Although I was conscious of my daily mounting unpaid debt to her, I often thought how true was Teacher Chen's advice that a friend was a treasure beyond price.

When the summer arrived, one wave of suffocating heat followed another, bringing thick clouds of mosquitoes, which made sitting outside at night impossible. The living conditions inside the ovenlike dorm were unbearable. We propped the windows open but, afraid of the prisoners, we locked the doors when we were sleeping, so there was little air circulation. Although we had managed to persuade the committee to allow us to break up the long trestle bed into separate doubles so that we could more easily hang our separate mosquito nets, nothing relieved the heat. Almost everyone was covered with heat rash as well as skin afflictions caused by the fertilizers we spread by hand in the paddies.

There was no bath- or shower-house, but I was able to wash in the nearby river. Not everyone was so lucky; the others feared the river because they couldn't swim. Bathing in the warm river water reminded me of the day when the news came to Shanghai that seventy-three-year-old Chairman Mao had swum in the Yangtze. The city government had organized the citizens on numerous occasions to emulate Mao by swimming in the polluted Huangpu River. I had joined Number 2 and his factory team, but suffered severe diarrhea after swallowing a couple of mouthfuls of polluted water. On the farm, I was more careful.

—

As a reward for their work in rice transplanting, Lao Chang had always allowed the prisoners to catch fish by blocking off a section of the river. So in early August, they built dikes to partition the river; then, with wooden barrels, they bailed the water out of the temporary pond. It was a round-the-clock operation for a day or so until the water was shallow enough to wade in and grab the fish. This year, instead of handing the catch over to the canteen immediately, they secretly stored the fish in barrels until it began to rot.

Then, to our surprise, one day our canteen was presented with a load of cleaned fish covered with salt. The salt was to keep the fish fresh, the prisoners explained. Inexperienced and ignorant, the staff washed off the salt and sent out the news that we were to receive a treat that night. We were delighted. Fish is always a delicacy; to us, living as we did on boring and often inadequate food, it was a gift from the gods. There was a long lineup before the canteen opened.

By midnight the doctor and his assistant were run ragged making trips from dorm to dorm, cleaning up vomit and caring for those who rolled on the floor clutching their abdomens. Everyone was on the move, either to or from the latrines or helping out the doctors and patients. When the morning arrived, hardly a student was able to get out of bed.

I was hit hard. After a night of violent cramps, vomiting and running to the latrine, my whole body felt like a cotton ball, totally without energy. I craved water but was afraid to drink. By noon the sub-farm medical team had arrived, bringing large quantities of antibiotics. But they were too late. The latrines soon contaminated our water supply, and before we had recovered from the food poisoning, we were in deeper trouble with severe diarrhea. On the fifth day I and three other girls were so dehydrated that we were taken to the farm hospital more than fifteen kilometres away in a flatbed wagon pulled by a water buffalo. Because I passed out, I remember nothing of the trip. My condition worsened. My body was wracked with pain and I was continuously voiding bloody feces.

Diagnosed with amoebic dysentery by a mobile medical team from Shanghai Number 1 People's Hospital, I was rushed by jeep to the ship, then to Shanghai dock, and from there directly to hospital. I was told my life was in danger unless I received proper medical treatment immediately. After two days in hospital the doctor said, "You have escaped Death's hand, but barely. Your disease will likely recur." For the next week I continued my frequent visits to the toilet, but could not eat. Instead I received glucose injections. When I was released, I weighed less than seventy pounds.

I had ached to see Purple Sunshine Lane and my family, so much so that I was almost grateful for my illness, despite its severity. Great-Aunt and Number 2 came to take me home in a taxi, an unheard-of luxury and the first such experience of my life. I had every reason to be cheerful, considering that I was still alive, but I found myself pensive and sad. In the nine months since I had left, the city had become a huge construction site, with clouds of dust in the air and piles of dirt along every road. As the taxi passed through the streets, my brother told me that after the military clashes with the Soviet Union over Zhenbao—Treasure—Island in the Heilongjiang River which separated the two countries, the whole nation was gearing up for war. Every work unit and neighbourhood committee was responsible for its own air-raid shelters. Mao's call had been for "deep digging [shelters], massive saving [of grain] and no dealings with the superpowers [since the U.S. and Russia were both against us]." While the young continued to be sent out to the countryside, tens of thousands of government employees were "evacuated" to rural areas and remote provinces to decentralize industry so that it would not all be destroyed if the cities were hit with air raids.

Following Mao's new policy, both Number 1 and Number 5 had been forced to leave the city in July, and I hadn't been allowed to go home to see them off. Number 5, after spending less than a year at middle school, left as a "graduate" and was sent to an army reclamation farm in Jiangxi Province, southeast of Shanghai. My eldest brother, a student of motor vehicle engineering, was assigned to a tool-repair shop in a small town in Guizhou Province, one of the poorest and most backward areas of the country. His letters confirmed the frequent rumour that "some people in Guizhou are so destitute that the whole family shares one pair of pants."

Thinking about Number 5 and Number 1 added to my depression. Our family was scattered now, their intelligence and abilities wasted. When I thought of my mother's anguish at having to decide which one of her sons would get a university education, my heart was heavy. Number 1 had gone to university only to be banished to a wasteland.

As if that was not enough, when we had a chance to talk alone Number 2 informed me that Number 3 had not been home from Songjiang for months.

"I have to explain this to you before you ask after her," he began. "For the past months Great-Aunt's resentment toward Number 3 for letting you go to the countryside has made Great-Aunt hostile and abusive. She accused Number 3 of being a coward and the worst kind of elder sister. Ah Si, we all are aware that you made a huge sacrifice for the family, but Number 3 has not had an easy time since you left. She could hardly keep a dry eye whenever you were mentioned and the tremendous burden will go with her for the rest of her life, even without Great-Aunt's blame. What a time!" he sighed. "You have a home that you are not *free* to visit, and Number 3 has one that she is *afraid* to visit!"

How could Great-Aunt say things like that to someone who had spent her entire first month's salary to buy me a fashionable polyester shirt, much prized in China at that time? But my resentment toward Great-Aunt—whom I had missed greatly—was, as usual, tinged with guilt. I understood why she treated my sister badly. I wished she could treat all of us equally, but it was not in her nature.

Lying in the darkness on my first night at home after almost a year, I was torn apart with conflicting loyalties, and my tears ran down onto the pillow. After living in pretense for the past ten months mouthing political slogans, now I had to hide my feelings at home too.

Number 3 came home to Purple Sunshine Lane a few days later. She burst into tears when I opened the door, skinny and wasted from my illness and all the hard work. "Great-Aunt was right," she exclaimed. "This is my fault!" She asked me a thousand questions and I tried my best to answer them without including the grim details. I turned the food poisoning into a humorous episode; the dysentery I reported as a character-building life-experience. Telling the truth would do no one any good.

I tried to reconcile Number 3 and Great-Aunt but the effort was in vain. Great-Aunt ignored my sister but doted on me, doing my laundry, cooking my favourite dishes, offering

me money to see a movie or go shopping. But she never sat
and talked with me. She kept herself busy all the time, playing her part in the massive earth-digging campaign during the
day, distributing mosquito pesticide on behalf of the neighbourhood committee at night. "The worst year for mosquitoes
I have ever experienced," she said.

After four weeks, during which I spent most of my time
alone in our apartment, the doctor stopped my sick leave and
Great-Aunt took to her flour roasting again. How I wished
that time could stop, or at least slow down. With every revolution of Great Aunt's spoon as she stirred the flour, my sense of
helplessness and despair increased. Before me the endless days
of labour and loneliness waited north of the Yangtze River.

But, too soon, the last morning dawned. Number 2 and
Number 3 saw me off at the dock, and I was on my way to the
Da Feng Prison Farm once more.

CHAPTER FIFTEEN

—

I returned to the farm early in October to find that the People's Liberation Army had taken over—specifically, the air force, which was loyal to Chairman Mao's right-hand man, Vice Chairman Lin Biao, and his son, Lin Li-guo, who had been named deputy commander. The PLA representatives had established themselves at leading levels of the farm, sub-farm and brigade.

Our brigade's two reps made an interesting team. They were both officers, but there the similarity ended. Cui was in his thirties, slim, average height, appearing reasonable and well-spoken. Zhao was in his forties, chunky and strong. Everything about him was short, from his arms and legs to his almost invisible neck. After only a few days I concluded that the big head that sat on that neck was hollow.

If Cui had earned his four officer's pockets by his charm
and elementary-school education, the unschooled and illiterate Zhao had acquired his by sweating, and even shedding
blood, for twenty years. The two of them reminded me of
the "red face" and "white face" characters in classical plays,
such as the traditional Beijing Opera, in which a red-painted
face represents a good person while the white denotes its
opposite, though quite often they worked together. From the
beginning Cui and Zhao worked that way.

Zhao described himself to us as *lao-da-cu*—old, big and
inelegant. Unlike us, he pointed out, who had drunk a few
bottles of ink so that we had more twists in our minds than in
our guts, making us hard to deal with, he was simple and
direct. Red-face Cui would then take over, saying that he himself had a mind no different from ours, so we would get along
just fine. Zhao liked to yell and shout to emphasize his
remarks; Cui spoke in a low voice and sometimes joked
around while conveying the same message.

Some of us felt they were a two-man comedy show, but
their routine filled me with unease. Why did they act that way
instead of being straightforward?

At that time I and others held the PLA in the highest possible esteem. They were the heroic "uncles" who had brought
Liberation: self-sacrificing men and women who loved China
and Chairman Mao. Even the Cultural Revolution had not
smeared them. Their rigid "Three Main Rules and Eight
Points of Attention" were well known to every schoolchild.
(Obey orders in all actions; take not even a single needle or

piece of thread from the citizens; turn in everything captured—these were the three rules. Speak politely; pay fairly for what you buy; return everything you borrow; compensate for anything you damage; swear at or hit no one; damage no crops; take no liberties with women; mistreat no captives—these were the eight points.) Mao had recently called upon the whole nation to learn from the revered PLA. In the days to come I would have a hard time relating what I had been taught at school to what I saw with my own eyes.

A brick house was under construction on the south side of our village to house Cui and Zhao and their office. No wattle and thatch for them. We female labourers were divided into teams of four, given a cart and sent to the sub-farm for bricks. The long flatbed cart with projecting handles and a straw pull-rope bounced easily over the deep ruts left by the typhoons. But once loaded with bricks it became as difficult to handle as an angry water buffalo. With one person on each handle, one shouldering the pull-rope and the last one pushing from the rear, we were barely able to move the cart and wept with frustration when the two lost control of the handles and the rear of the cart slammed to the ground, throwing the bricks into the road. When we finally reached our destination we were mocked by the bricklayers for bringing hardly enough bricks to make a thin pillar.

The very day that our PLA reps moved into their eye-catching new house, Lao Chang rushed us back to the paddies, where the rice stalks had turned golden yellow. Although our paddies were nothing like the "rolling waves of golden ears" described in songs, we were excited because we knew that every single plant had been touched by our hands, from gently tugging the seedlings from their beds, to planting them in straight rows, to endless weedings and applications of fertilizer. Now the rice would be cut down, by hand.

The paddies had been drained and harvesting could begin; once again Lao Chang reminded us that timing was everything. For two weeks we worked from dawn until dark. Our lunches were brought to the fields so that we would lose no time. Wearing boots (the paddies were still muddy) and a long-sleeved shirt to protect my forearms from the rough stalks, I wielded my sickle, bent at the waist, hour after hour, chopping the plants off at ground level and piling them carefully so that they could be bundled up and hauled away to the threshing ground.

After each day of bone-weary labour we still had to endure political study at night. Although we never saw Cui and Zhao during the day—they were rushing between meetings in their jeep, often accompanied by two lucky and usually good-looking female students chosen to take notes for them—they always showed up for political study. And both of them had "elephant bottoms," for when the endless meetings finally drew to a close, they seemed reluctant to leave our dorm. None of us could get ready for bed while they were there. They never seemed interested in conducting political study with the men.

In November the threshing began. This was a new experience for me and it soon proved horrifying. This year the women had no help, for all the male labourers, including the prisoners, had been commandeered to rebuild the main road. "Order Number 1" had reached the farm, Zhao told us at the meeting: "Our great leader Chairman Mao teaches us to 'be prepared for war and natural disaster.' The original road is not adequate for military vehicles."

While trucks loaded with gravel and cement rumbled to and fro, throwing up clouds of dust, we worked at the threshing ground, a large flat area trampled hard and free of vegetation. Six horizontal thresher barrels were turned by long belts attached to an electric motor. From the surface of the barrels projected long, sharp metal teeth. As the drum turned, I held a bundle of rice against the top so that the teeth could tear the ears free. One careless move and my hand would be ripped to shreds. It would be even worse if I fell against the swiftly revolving barrel.

Once threshed, the bundles of rice stalks were stacked for later use in building, rope making and so on. On the other side of the barrels, where the ears fell, workers raked away the chaff. It would be used for fuel. Everyone wore a cotton mask against the cloud of dust that hung in the air so thickly that it almost obscured the lights set up for the evening shifts.

I found it impossible to hold the bundle of rice stalks against the barrel in the prescribed manner because my "kindling arms" were not strong enough and the bundle was often yanked from my hands. I tried to compensate by wrapping my arms around the bundle and pressing it against my chest. This method required that I lean closer to the whirling, flashing teeth. Even worse, since I was too short, Lao Chang ordered me to stand on a pile of straw, making balance all the more difficult to maintain.

For the first few nights I had nightmares about falling against the barrel and being shredded to bloody bits. I wasn't sure whether it was my pleas or the fact that I would often lose my hold on the bundle and watch helplessly as it was torn from my arms and pulled under the barrel, causing the whole production line to come to a halt, but Lao Chang eventually reassigned me to pile up the threshed bundles.

Thus the first anniversary of my coming to the farm rolled around. It was Jia-ying who reminded me of the date. But what use was it to remember?

—

I had never bought Great-Aunt's theory that I was a girl born with bad luck, but occasionally I wondered. One sunny day during our lunch break, I fell to the threshing ground with a sharp pain in my abdomen. The pain grew and I was soaked in sweat, curled up like a shrimp. Yu Hua immediately sent someone to the road-construction site for Dr. Wang. Lao Chang arrived but could do nothing except stand there and make guesses. A while later Dr. Wang ran up with two young men, Xiao Zhu and Xiao Qian, who carried a stretcher between them. It took the doctor only a few moments of prodding my stomach to diagnose acute appendicitis.

"You need an operation," he urged. "Immediately. We must get you to a hospital."

Xiao Zhu and Xiao Qian wrapped me in quilts and put me onto a cart, the kind we had used to haul bricks. There were no proper medical facilities in our village nor on the sub-farm; worse, because the main road was under construction, the farm hospital couldn't send its ambulance over. So Dr. Wang took the lead and the two men followed, one pulling, the other pushing along the rutted country road to the Sanlong—Three Dragon—River, which bordered a commune about two kilometres away. The distance seemed like the Long March, as every bump and shudder of the cart sent a searing arrow of pain through my belly. Yu Hua periodically mopped the cold sweat off my brow as she jogged alongside.

The Sanlong River was about fifty metres wide, broader and cleaner than the tributary that flowed beside our road, and marked the boundary of the commune which, because of constant raids by prisoners who stole crops and animals to supplement their meagre diets, was like an armed camp surrounded by a wire fence.

It was about two o'clock when we reached the river. Dr. Wang and the two men called across for help. There was no response. Yu Hua began to run along the bank, jumping and shouting in her surprisingly deep voice. "It's an emergency! Please help us!"

Sweat bathed my face and soaked my clothes. Scared, still curled tight, knees to my chest and chin tucked in, I fought the nausea and piercing jabs of pain. Yu Hua's frantic calls and the doctor's urgent commands did little to dispel my anxiety.

Finally a voice floated across the river. "Wait a bit. We're sending a boat over."

Xiao Qian and Xiao Zhu carried my stretcher onto a barge. The doctor and Yu Hua scrambled aboard and we were poled across. Another cart was found and the painful jouncing began again.

By the time I was in the operating room night had fallen. Dr. Wang was beside me. I wished desperately that someone from my family were present. I knew nothing about appendicitis and its possible complications. All I knew was that Dr. Wang was going to cut me open and I might die.

I had been put under only local anesthetic, so I was fully aware of what was happening. I could see nothing but the ceiling but heard the clink of surgical instruments dropped onto trays and the rustle of clothing. There were two other doctors, constantly asking Dr. Wang questions and criticizing him about the delay. No one wanted to talk to me, apparently.

Then everything went black.

"Doctor, help! I've gone blind!" I cried out.

Curses rang out in the pitch darkness. Feet shuffled.

"No, no, Xiao Ye," Dr. Wang said. "The electricity went off. Don't worry, the nurses are out looking for flashlights. Thank goodness I have already removed your inflamed appendix."

Losing electricity was not new to me or to anyone else in China. Even in Shanghai, power was regularly cut off in residential areas on certain days to conserve energy. Factories sometimes sent an entire shift home, especially during the summer, a time of peak consumption. But there was usually a warning.

The nurses soon returned, barely visible behind the bobbing orbs of their flashlights. I closed my eyes again, completely spent, only to open them wide when a sharp pain shot through my stomach, causing my right leg to recoil. The anesthetic had worn off. Someone pushed my leg down and I realized the operation was still going on. I screamed when another bolt of pain went through me.

"What's wrong! What are you doing to me?"

"It's all right," one of the nurses said calmly, "the doctor is sewing you up. He shouldn't be long."

I screamed for more anaesthetic.

"Not possible," Dr. Wang said. "The needle would have to be administered in your spine and we can't turn you over."

Holding her flashlight to illuminate her little red book, a nurse started to read quotations from Chairman Mao. "Do not fear hardship; do not fear death," she urged.

When Chairman Mao penned that advice, I doubted he was being repeatedly punctured by a sewing needle. I gritted my teeth against the pain. The nurse recited more useless advice.

Finally, I was carried on a stretcher into the dimly lit ward, completely drained but out of danger. Yu Hua and the two young men who had brought me all that way were waiting to see how I had fared in the operation. I was deeply touched by their kindness and I wanted to thank them, but all I could manage was a weak smile.

CHAPTER SIXTEEN

—

I was released from the hospital a week later and given light duty cleaning up in the canteen. I felt lucky to be working indoors, for the northwest wind had turned sharply cold again and the dampness chilled us to the bone. The male students were still labouring to complete the road and the women were building paddy dikes with heavy iron-toothed rakes. If the dikes were not made properly, Cui or Zhao squashed them flat and ordered them redone.

Failure to reach quotas no longer brought a simple minus sign on the posted list. It was now considered to be politically motivated, and that meant trouble. After the PLA's arrival, everything was done the military way. We were no longer allowed to walk to the canteen individually, "like a plate of loose sand," as Cui put it. As "real soldiers" we marched together, bowls in our left hands, swinging our right arms in unison. Students with red family backgrounds were formed into a militia with daily training, including rifle practice, led by Zhao. The militia was on call twenty-four hours a day.

On call for what? Although I had never been a "news digger," I had never been so ill-informed as I had been since coming to the farm. There was no newspaper available, and transistor radios, at that time rare and expensive, provided only repetitive propaganda because all media in China was state-controlled. Needless to say, the camp's loudspeakers offered the same. Even though mail was delivered twice a week, everyone knew that putting things down in black and white in such dangerous times was not a good idea. I was aware only of what was going on in our little village.

As I had seen during my medical leave in Shanghai a few months earlier, the whole country was building air-raid shelters because of the conflict with Russia, but why did our farm need a "ready for war" road, broad and strong enough, in Zhao's words, for two tanks to travel side by side? And why did we need a militia? What strategic importance could our village have, out in the middle of nowhere, surrounded by flat land that produced poor crops?

As winter deepened, we looked forward to a few relatively easy months before spring brought back the intensive heavy labour of growing rice. The temperature dropped so low that on some mornings we found the water jars sealed with ice. To stay warm at night when the wind hissed through the wattle walls of our unheated dorm, Yu Hua and I put our bedding together, as did others.

But many was the time we were torn from our sleep by the sharp ringing of bells calling us to military exercises. Militia members or not, we all had to go, jumping out of our beds into the freezing darkness, fumbling into our clothes, dashing to the threshing grounds to be harangued by Cui and Zhao, snug and warm in their army greatcoats, peering at their stop-watches. I had accepted hard labour long ago, but I hated the "war preparation."

One night at our regular political study meeting, a few women were talking about the cost of building the road, trading rumours and passing on gossip.

"All that effort and expense to build a road nobody uses," I joked. "Too bad we couldn't put half the time and money into building dorms with thicker walls."

That remark would come back to haunt me.

When February rolled around the students' spirits lifted, for it was time for *tan-qin*—home visit—the national govern-ment policy of a two-week paid holiday each year for employees who worked away from home. Travel costs were picked up by the work unit. Lao Chang had told us long ago that we could take our *tan-qin* at any time during the year, except busy seasons, but Cui had changed that, saying we must all go home at the same time.

Lately, I had been worried about Number 5. In her letters she sounded so depressed that I was afraid she was heading for a nervous breakdown. Each letter ripped my heart to

pieces. I had planned to wait and take my *tan-qin* in July to
coincide with hers so that I could meet her at home. Cui's new
policy ruined my plans.

When I asked Yu Hua what I should do, she suggested I
explain things to Cui and Zhao. "You have reasonable grounds
for an exception," she advised. "I am your squad leader. I'll go
with you to talk to them."

That night we went to the brick building and knocked on
the door. The reps' office was lit by two bare bulbs hanging
from the ceiling. Cui and Zhao sat at their respective desks,
sipping tea, their faces blank.

I was so nervous that I tripped over my words, so Yu Hua
stepped in to explain that both my parents were dead and that
I had hoped to take my vacation at the same time as my siblings. "They have been scattered," she finished, "and want to see
each other when they can."

"If I can take my two weeks later on," I said weakly, "I promise to work all the harder when I return."

Cui and Zhao sat silent, as if we were not there, as if neither of us had said a word. I recalled the humiliation I felt on
my many visits with Mother to uncaring factory officials who
offered no financial help after Father died. Suddenly I missed
both my parents terribly and began to cry.

Cui stood up and came around to the front of his desk. A
cold smile crossed his face. "What are you crying for?" he said
harshly. "We haven't said a word yet, have we?"

He smirked at Zhao, who was leafing through the registration book that held all our names and family histories.

"*Tan-qin* is for comrades who are married and working away from their spouses, or for unmarried ones to visit their parents. Isn't it?"

"Yes, Representative Zhao," I muttered.

"Are you married?" he asked with phony politeness. Cui smirked.

"No, Representative Zhao."

"Then you have no spouse to visit, do you? And your parents are dead. So it seems," he concluded, "that you are not eligible for *tan-qin* at all."

I turned cold with fear. I would never see my brothers and sisters or Great-Aunt again.

Zhao stood up, his face still calm, his voice restrained. "There are millions of brothers and sisters sent to different places to serve our motherland. Why should you get special treatment? You of all people," he added, "with your black class background."

My lips trembled. I looked at my friend. Yu Hua's expression told me she was as astonished as I.

"Please," I managed, but Cui cut me off, laughing.

"We'll let you know. You're not in a hurry, of course. You said you wanted to delay your visit. And your parents won't be in a hurry, will they?" He laughed even louder. "The two of you are dismissed."

I was so scared I couldn't sleep that night, and the next morning, Yu Hua tried to console me, but failed. Then she brightened. "Xiao Ye, I have an idea. Let's go to the sub-farm administrative office and get this cleared up. Cui and Zhao are low level, after all. They shouldn't be interfering in this matter."

Once again I was grateful for my friend's clear head. After we hurried to finish our quota of new paddy dikes, we asked Jia-ying to fetch our supper for us and keep it in the dorm, then headed for the sub-farm. By the time we arrived, it was dark. My heart fell when I saw the office was closed for the day.

"Don't give up," Yu Hua urged. "Maybe they're having supper."

We found the canteen and, after questioning a number of people, were directed toward a tall, middle-aged man eating alone at one of the tables. PLA representative Huang, who was army, not air force, had a kindly face and large, intelligent eyes. Hearing the reason for our visit, he led us to his office.

His accent placed him from Zhejiang Province. He invited us to sit down, and his politeness gave me confidence. I omitted my original request to delay my *tan-qin* until July. I explained my concern that the reps might not allow me to go home at all. Representative Huang took out his copy of the farm personnel registration book, leafed through it, turned it toward me, and asked me to point out my name. I did so, with a shaking finger. He read the information about my family, then closed the book and looked up.

"There will be no problem," he said. He went on to explain that the government policy applied to everyone. As he spoke, an angry edge crept into his voice. "It is tragic enough that you lost both your parents. How could those two—" and he stopped himself.

On our way back to our village, we met Xiao Zhu, Xiao Qian and Xiao Jian, three male friends of Yu Hua. Zhu and

Qian were the ones who had helped during my attack of appendicitis, and all three of them, along with Yu Hua, had visited me in the hospital. I had always appreciated their friendliness. Like Yu Hua, they were all older than me, but despite their correct political backgrounds, none of them looked down on me.

Xiao Jian—the young assistant accountant—suggested we all go to his tiny office next to the canteen where he could heat up our supper. While I ate, I talked and laughed, happy that my problem had been solved and delighting in their camaraderie.

The next evening Yu Hua and I were summoned to Cui and Zhao's office. As soon as we entered, Zhao began to shout at us.

"How dare you two play tricks behind our backs!" he screamed, his face red with anger. "How dare you go over our heads!"

Swearing and cursing, his cap crooked on his head, he accused us of trying to undermine the PLA. When we tried to speak he cut us off, became angrier, screamed louder. Cui sat at his desk playing with a pencil, not saying a word through the entire tirade, until he finally dismissed us with a wave of his hand.

"Screw your mothers!" Zhao shouted as we left. "Screw both of them!"

We slunk away. I had no idea what kind of a mistake we had made, but when I boarded the ship for Shanghai a week later, my heart was full of foreboding. I knew I had not heard the last from Cui and Zhao.

—

The dock at Shanghai Number 16 Pier was awash in people. Shouts of joy swirled around me as my farm-mates threw themselves into the arms of weeping mothers and fathers. No one from my family was there to greet me. Great-Aunt, now almost sixty, was too old to fight the crowds; on her three-inch lily feet she would have been thrown off balance and trampled in no time. Number 1's and Number 5's *tan-qin* did not coincide with mine. Number 2 would be home soon, but this day he was digging air-raid shelters in the suburbs with his fellow workers. Number 3 couldn't get to the city until Sunday, her day off.

Since I knew I would find the apartment that once rang with the noise and bustle of eight people empty and quiet, I was in no hurry to get home. I also knew that as soon as I walked in the door I would start to pretend, for I couldn't burden anyone with my true experiences and loneliness on the farm. I stood in the cold February rain waiting for my bus.

—

Number 3's arrival in Purple Sunshine Lane lifted my heart.

"Ah Si, you look wonderful," she exclaimed as soon as she came in the door. "The last time I saw you, you were as thin as a stick!"

A pretty young woman, now nineteen, she lived in a one-room factory dorm with three other unmarried female workers—not an ideal arrangement, but her job meant she was secure from assignment to the countryside and could think about settling down.

Over tea prepared by Great-Aunt, we chatted happily.

"I haven't found a boyfriend yet, but I've got my eye open," Number 3 joked. "Look," she added proudly, handing me a photograph that showed her in an army uniform, a gun slung over her shoulder.

"You're in the militia?" I asked, passing the photo to Great-Aunt.

"I'm a leader!"

"By the time Number 3 gets around to pointing her gun," Great-Aunt put in caustically, "the Russians will have taken over the factory."

"I'm surprised they accepted the daughter of a capitalist," I said.

(Left) Number 1 disguised as a Red Guard in the "Great Travels," 1966, in front of the Yangtze River Bridge in Wuhan.
(Right) Number 3, an enthusiastic member of her factory militia, in Songjiang County, 1969.

Number 1 (with clarinet) rehearsing with the Spreading Mao Ze-dong Thought Band, 1966.

"Oh, they don't care. I don't give them any trouble. Eat, sleep and work, that's my motto."

A few days later, when I told Number 2 about almost having had my *tan-qin* taken away, he explained the new political climate to me, and some of the strange things on the farm began to make sense. When Mao had ordered the PLA into the work units to stabilize them against further upheavals and civil strife, the plan had been to establish "three-in-one" authority, composed of representatives from the masses, the Party officials and the PLA. Since then the PLA had accumulated more and more authority in farms, factories and bureaucracies, and once this power was firmly established, it had launched a purge of those who were against its involvement. The strongest

anti-PLA voices came from universities and academic insti-
tutes; consequently, a "counterrevolutionary" group was
"discovered" at the famous Fudan University in Shanghai. A
wide-ranging witch-hunt followed.

This situation was further complicated, as I learned many
years later, because Lin Biao had long been quietly preparing
to overthrow Mao and take over the country. In total control
of the air force and much of the rest of the armed services, Lin
Biao was putting men loyal to him into key positions. When
the time was right, he planned to assassinate Mao Ze-dong
and take power. In retrospect, the reason for the new road on
our farm became clear. The road was not there to prepare for
a Russian invasion at all; it was there in case of civil war, to
support a possible retreat of Lin Biao's forces.

None of us then knew of Lin Biao's plot. All Number 2
understood was that the PLA had achieved new power in
China and was ferreting out all opposition. He warned me to
steer clear of any conflict, particularly where the PLA reps
were concerned.

Neither he nor I knew the full significance of my visit with
Yu Hua to see Representative Huang at the sub-farm, nor of
his intervention on my behalf. The sub-farm administration
office was, like all units, assigned PLA representatives: that
was Huang's function. But the sub-farm PLA reps were from
the Shanghai Garrison, which in turn was controlled by the
Nanjing Military Region, a force loyal to Chairman Mao, and
therefore hostile to Lin Biao. Thus, by going over Cui's and
Zhao's heads, Yu Hua and I had gone to their enemy.

CHAPTER SEVENTEEN

—

The evening after my return to the farm at the beginning of March, an urgent meeting was called in the warehouse. We were instructed not to bring our pens, notebooks and stools—an unprecedented announcement that made me nervous. In those days anything out of the ordinary was a bad omen, and Yu Hua and I were already in the reps' bad books.

The warehouse was festooned with political slogans. "Never Forget the Class Struggle!" "Forgetting Means Betrayal!" "Long Live the People's Liberation Army!" "We Will Smash the Heads of Anyone Who Dares to Oppose the Army!" I was well used to the strident tone of posters, but this last seemed unusually threatening.

Once inside the cold, damp warehouse, we were directed to sit on the freezing cement floor, not to squat on our heels. Cui was in his glory. Fist in the air, he led the recitation of Chairman Mao's slogan, "Grasp class struggle and all problems can be solved!" It grew louder with each repetition. As the room boomed and echoed with the well-worn words, two white-clad canteen staff walked slowly to the front, a huge wok held between them. Ceremoniously, they placed the wok on the ground at Cui's feet.

Cui motioned for silence, tugged at the tails of his jacket, and began to speak. "Representative Zhao and I feel that there is a lack of class-struggle consciousness in our brigade. Chairman Mao has taught us that the class struggle must continue! In order to carry the Great Proletarian Cultural Revolution through to the end, it is necessary for all of us to be reminded of the proletariat's hardships before Liberation."

I eyed the wok as an unpleasant smell spread through the chilly warehouse.

"We are going to have a special meal," Cui went on, pointing at the wok, "to recall the suffering of the past so that we can appreciate the good life of the present. I warn you, Representative Zhao and I will be watching carefully to make sure all of you take part. Any cheating will be considered politically motivated."

One by one we filed to the front to get our share of the "meal." When it was my turn I was handed a fist-sized ball of malodorous, lukewarm green stuff. I returned to my place, sat down and regarded the repulsive object that was to put me in touch with the pre-Liberation poor. The ball was heavy and smelled of earth and grass. I glanced at Yu Hua, who shrugged her shoulders and tried not to show her disgust. I broke it in two, but long green stringy stuff bound the halves together.

"Come on!" came Zhao's voice. "Don't be cowardly. Remember some of your former generations had even less to eat. Of course, others had an easy life sucking the blood of the poor!"

I held my breath, closed my eyes and took a bite. The ball had a sandy, rubbery consistency and tasted of hot bitter grass and foul dirt. It seemed to be made of weeds mixed with wheat chaff. The stringy texture and horrible odour made me gag.

Poor Jia-ying, who sat near me, threw up hard, soiling her jacket and the cement floor in front of her. The smell of her vomit didn't make my task any easier.

Yu Hua leaned over. "Break it into pieces with your finger-nails and swallow the bits. Don't chew it."

Jia-ying was weeping in frustration. Each time she put the putrid green ball to her mouth she vomited again. She begged Zhao for some water, but he walked away. For me Yu Hua's method worked, and within a few moments I had forced the pieces down my throat. I slipped closer to Jia-ying and told her what to do. Finally, she too succeeded and, through her tears, she smiled with relief.

As we left the warehouse we passed two inspectors who made us open our mouths, lift up our tongues, and then turn out our pockets. I was convinced the sadistic display by Cui and Zhao had one purpose only: to show us they could do whatever they wanted with us.

I tossed and turned all night, my stomach aching, until dawn was ushered in by a voice blasting from the loudspeakers, commanding the entire camp to another meeting after dinner. Marching to the canteen that night, we passed a bunch of prisoners who had gathered to torment us. With bits of grass and straw protruding from their mouths, they laughed and jeered at us. One lay on the ground, twitching, as if seized by epilepsy.

"Ignore them," Cui warned us. "When you look at them, you see nothing."

In many ways I felt that the prisoners had more freedom than us and their lives were easier, since they were not required to participate in the Cultural Revolution. And when they had served their time, they would go back to their families. Three months short of my eighteenth birthday, I knew my sentence was final, for life. Some of the male students on the farm had run away, hoping they would be caught and sent over to the prisoners' section, but they were returned to the brigade. It was, to me, part of the madness of the Cultural Revolution that lawbreakers were better off than people who had done nothing wrong.

That night, Cui took a different tack at the meeting. He cajoled us, humbly asking for our help. "Representative Zhao and I are relatively new here and inexperienced at this kind of work," he said with false sincerity. "We are unfamiliar with sophisticated city youth. Please help us by writing your criticisms and suggestions. Be open and honest; in this way you can show your support for the PLA."

Remembering Number 2's warnings, I determined to do and say nothing. I advised Yu Hua to act the same way. But she was taken in. She wrote a criticism of Cui and Zhao, saying that, in dealing with my request to reschedule my *tan-qin*, they had behaved unfairly.

Three days later, the two PLA reps proved they had learned well from the "Hundred Flowers" movement in 1957 when Mao had rounded up those who had naively penned the criticisms he had requested. The reps even used Mao's words in their posters: "The Snake Has Poked Its Head Out of the Hole: What Shall We Do About It?" "Those Who Try to Overthrow the PLA Will Have No Good End!" Other *da-zi-bao* encouraged the students to expose those who opposed Cui and Zhao behind each other's backs.

Depressed and disheartened, I tried to prepare my mind for the attacks, the suspicion and the betrayals to come. Outside the dorm, a bitter northwest wind howled.

CHAPTER EIGHTEEN

—

A witch-hunt was launched in our brigade. From among the "red" students an eight-member "examine and uncover team" was formed, its members relieved of all other duties. They were to help Cui and Zhao carry out the purge. The three women chosen for this team were Loaf, Fatty and Leggy, nicknamed, like many of us, according to their appearance. Loaf, whose eyeglasses were the thickest I had ever seen, was proud that her father, a tailor, was making costumes for the modern ballet "The White-Haired Girl," one of only eight plays Jiang Qing allowed to be publicly performed. Fatty often voiced the revolution's bloodline theory that "a dragon's son is a dragon." Needless to say, her blood ran pure. Tall and slender, with a large, flat head, Leggy was a hard worker who kept to herself. She had denounced her whole family after her father was labelled a rightist and had since been chosen as a model youth. Leggy even gave up her *tan-qin*, refusing to visit her "politically muddle-headed mother." I did not know the rest of the team well, but soon found that they were equally malevolent.

I was horrified to learn that the "snake's head" that had, according to Cui and Zhao, shown itself by coming part way out of its hole was the foursome who had befriended me when I was ill and when I returned from the sub-farm office to inquire about my home leave. They were Yu Hua, my friend and protector, Xiao Zhu, Xiao Qian and Xiao Jian. All four were from correct class backgrounds, and all were leaders. But all were naive. They had, as requested by Cui, written and turned in their criticisms and suggestions.

At the "struggle meeting" that followed, my four friends were forced to stand before us as Cui led the crowd in shouting and waving fists, demanding that they confess their crimes.

"They have been hiding behind a curtain!" he screamed. "They and anyone who is part of their counterrevolutionary plot must be exposed!"

The din created by the hollering, in which I didn't participate, almost split my eardrums. My friends stood with heads bowed, humiliated and looking guilty. It was too ridiculous to think that they had plotted to undermine the revolution and the PLA.

After more bellowed slogans, more urging to expose the snakes and all who crawled with them, Cui ended the meeting by announcing that the four were now under house arrest.

The crowd dutifully cheered and stamped their feet. My friends were led out of the warehouse, each followed by a "watcher" whose job was to stay with the person at all times.

I rushed back to my dorm to find Yu Hua packing her belongings. "Yu Hua, where are they taking you?"

"Shut up or you'll have to bear the consequences of talking to a counterrevolutionary!" shouted Fatty, her watcher.

Yu Hua, her eyes bright with fear, shook her head to indicate I should be quiet. I turned and asked the others in the dorm where my friend was being taken, but they had been intimidated into silence. I looked on as Yu Hua was led to the brick house.

Jia-ying appeared beside me. "Don't cry, Xiao Ye," she whispered. "The reps are simply killing a chicken to scare the monkeys. When you wake up, Yu Hua will be back."

I wished I could share her confidence.

—

I was shaken violently from a troubled sleep.

"Ye Ting-xing! Wake up! Get out of bed right now!"

Leggy and Fatty stood beside my bed, barely recognizable in the dim light.

"What's the matter? What time is it?"

Up and down the row, heads popped up; some girls leaned on their arms, staring at me.

"It's one o'clock," Jia-ying complained as Fatty threw my padded jacket into my face.

"Hurry up," Leggy commanded. "You're wanted by the reps. Right now!"

I struggled into my padded trousers, pulled on my socks and grabbed my coat. "Why do they want me in the middle of the night?"

"Hurry up," Leggy said again. "There is no limousine waiting for you, Miss! Stop dragging your feet."

The two of them bustled me out into the cold darkness. I tripped and stumbled repeatedly, for in my panic and haste I hadn't brought Number 2's glasses with me. There were a few people hanging around on the porch when we got to the brick house. Every light was on and the radio blared songs and quotations from Chairman Mao. Leggy pushed me inside.

Cui and Zhao were at their usual places behind their desks. I stood before them, shaking with fear.

"Do you know why you are here?" Zhao began.

I shook my head, squinting as my eyes accustomed themselves to the bright lights.

Zhao spoke calmly. "We have uncovered a counterrevolutionary group in this brigade, as you learned earlier tonight," he said. "We want to know about the meetings you have had with them. The times and locations of every gathering, every word spoken."

"I don't understand what you mean," I stammered.

"Don't play games with us," Zhao responded, maintaining his calm. "We know what's been going on. As a matter of fact, we are doing you a favour, giving you this chance to clear yourself."

"Clear myself from what? I don't know about any meetings."

In a flash Zhao slammed his hands on the desk and leapt to his feet, his face twisted with rage. "Our patience is limited," he shouted. "Don't try to stall. This is your only chance. Cooperate, or it will be too late for you!"

Cui too got to his feet, stepped around his desk and patted Zhao on the shoulder. Zhao took his seat.

With a phony smile on his face, Cui said patiently, "You see, your friends are under house arrest. We are treating you differently because we're confident that you'll help us. Think about it," he urged, pointing at the filing cabinets behind him. "You know your dossier is in there, and you know what it contains: three generations and more of your family's history. A family of landlords and capitalists."

I saw what Cui was implying. Everyone in China had a dossier; its importance was one of the first things I had learned as a young girl. Besides being used to brand you, the dossier contained every bit of damaging information anyone had said about you. The Red Guards had filled hundreds of thousands of dossiers with hatred and false information.

Cui and Zhao's plan now became clear to me. They considered me a member of the counterrevolutionary group—a group of five, not four. But because I was the only one with a bad class background, because I was the youngest, least experienced and most vulnerable, they thought I would break first and seize the opportunity to save myself by informing against the others.

Trembling, I clenched my fists and pressed my lips together. Cui ordered Fatty to take me into an adjoining room and guard me while I wrote a confession.

"No confession, no sleep," Zhao screamed as Fatty led me out.

In the small room, poorly illuminated by a single bulb hanging from the ceiling, were two desks and two stools. On one of the desks was a stack of paper and a pen. Fatty pushed me down on a stool.

"Write down everything you remember about your meetings with the others, as well as your own bad thoughts. Remember Chairman Mao's teachings, 'Leniency to those who confess their crimes, but severity to those who refuse.'"

She left the room, slamming the door. I sat there shaking, then for what seemed like hours just stared at the pen and paper.

The next thing I knew, Fatty was shouting, her face inches from mine. I must have fallen asleep. Others from the "examine and uncover" team were also yelling at me, criticizing my lack of co-operation. Finally, after repeated warnings, all but Fatty and Leggy left the room.

Until daylight showed in the window they took turns. I would stare at the blank paper until my eyes closed. A punch on my shoulder would snap me awake and I would try to focus on the page again.

Finally I wrote one sentence. "I, Ye Ting-xing, am sorry for being disrespectful to reps Cui and Zhao and I am willing to accept their punishment."

Fatty snatched the paper from my hands, then led me to breakfast. Mechanically I pushed food into my mouth while my watcher looked on silently. Immediately after, I was turned over to Loaf so that Fatty could catch some sleep, and escorted to the field. I was not permitted to sleep.

By this time I was like a zombie. A lost night of sleep was debilitating enough, but the fear and tension had drained all my energy. Once again I found myself the object of criticism and ridicule. I remembered Great-Aunt's expression: "We escaped the bitter sea only to fall into the mouth of a tiger." I worked alongside Yu Hua, building paddy dikes with a long heavy rake in the chilly late-March rain as our watchers sat chatting under umbrellas. We were not allowed to work with others, nor could we talk to each other. I was worried about Yu Hua. She was withdrawn, her eyes were puffy, and she seemed to have aged overnight. I wondered if I looked as bad.

That night yet another struggle meeting was held in the warehouse. When I walked in, trailed by Fatty, no one spoke to me. People looked away when I passed them. As soon as I sat down in the front row, someone yelled from the back, "Bring up the counterrevolutionaries!" Only then did I notice two cells made of bamboo poles and reed mats newly installed at each end of the warehouse. Yu Hua emerged from behind one of them. Xiao Jian, Xiao Qian and Xiao Zhu were led to sit behind me.

The same voice at the back began to chant slogans, and the crowd joined in. "Down with the counterrevolutionaries! Down with anyone who dares to oppose the PLA! Those who oppose the PLA are against the Communist Party!" With each deafening shout, my shoulders hunched a little more, as if the bitter words were being piled on my head. I glanced at my friends, who looked miserable and terrified. The whole scene brought back memories of Red Guards bellowing in the street outside our house in Purple Sunshine Lane.

The next stage of the struggle meeting was an open invitation for people to stand up and report on "crimes" committed by the five of us. One by one my friends were accused of betraying their class and of setting up a secret counterrevolutionary group.

When it came my turn, from behind me I heard, "Ye Ting-xing has no respect for the motherland! She makes fun of everything!"

"Ye Ting-xing looks down on the PLA," a second woman blurted out, referring to my mimicking of Zhao's Sichuan accent in the dorm at night. My joke about the new road, charged another, proved that my "hatred of our beloved PLA was rooted in my bad blood, which had been growing since the day I was born."

"Her parents were capitalists who sucked the blood of the working class," screamed a fourth.

The slanders, curses and insults went on and on, and my humiliation deepened with every lie or false accusation. How could all of them hate me so? I had never felt so alone. These were the women with whom I worked, ate and shared a dorm. If I could have, I would have ended my life there and then.

Finally Zhao stood up. The five of us had held secret meetings in Xiao Jian's tiny accounting office, he claimed. "You all know the size of that room," he sneered. "Just imagine how closely the five of them would have been jammed together. Do you really believe that they were just eating supper and talking?" He smirked, then pointing at Yu Hua and me. "And you two! You are constantly seen sharing the same bedding at night." He turned to the audience. "I wonder if staying warm was the only reason!"

His remark brought an uproar of laughter. From the corner of my eye I saw that Yu Hua had begun to cry. I knew nothing about lesbians, but Zhao's remark was clearly meant to be low and obscene, and I felt I would never hold up my head again.

CHAPTER NINETEEN

—

Two days later I was put under house arrest. Zhao had not been satisfied with my one-sentence confession. Loaf shoved me into the same room, pushed me behind the same desk and ordered me once again to confess all my crimes and report on the counterrevolutionary thoughts, words and actions of my four friends.

I didn't care any more. For the past two days I had not been shadowed because, as Cui put it, I was "under surveillance of the mobilized masses." The prisoners mocked me, the students lowered their eyes when I passed or openly criticized me. I felt like a leper.

There were two beds in the room, I noticed, one for me and one for Loaf. The first night was a repetition of my initial interrogation, shouting, punching, slapping whenever fatigue seemed to remove all the strength from my neck muscles. Fatty, Leggy and Loaf took turns: when one grew tired of the attack, another took over.

I wrote a few more sentences. I admitted to going over the heads of our PLA reps and criticized myself for doing so. At midnight I was allowed to lie down on the bed, fully clothed. Only minutes later, it seemed, I was shaken awake and dragged back to the desk.

"Not good enough," Loaf asserted. "Stop stalling. The reps say you're holding back. You must give a full confession."

"But I did nothing wrong," I repeated so often that it became a litany. "My friends did nothing wrong. We're not counterrevolutionaries!"

Shouting, stinging slaps on the face, criticism, insults. Back to bed. Shaken awake again. Pulled to the desk. More yelling, more demands.

Each morning I dragged myself to the paddies. Every evening there was another struggle meeting to vilify me and the other four "counterrevolutionaries" before I was hauled back to the room. Exhausted, disoriented and deprived of sleep, I finally wrote a full self-criticism, telling how I went to the sub-farm and what I said to Representative Huang about my *tan-qin*. I filled several pages, writing as much as I could to satisfy them. Anything to be allowed to sleep.

It wasn't enough. I was kicked awake again. By now I could no longer tell how long I had been allowed to doze. Was it four hours or four minutes? I lost track of how many days had passed since the interrogation had begun. Loaf hauled me back to my desk. Then Zhao came in, his military coat unbuttoned, his plastic slippers dragging. He sat beside me, very close, and ran his hand down the back of my head. I could smell green tea and cigarettes on his breath.

"Your hair needs a wash," he observed. Speaking softly, almost politely, in complete contrast to my watchers' aggressive abuse, he explained that my confession was a good start, very good indeed—but it didn't go far enough.

"You've told us what you did. But you must examine your thinking. What motivated you? What were you really attempting to do? Not simply talk about your home leave, surely? Wasn't there more to it? Think about it."

He left, closing the door quietly. I stared at the sheet of paper, struggling to keep my eyes open. The slam of a hand on the wood beside my ear startled me.

"Wake up, parentless bitch! Who gave you permission to sleep?"

"Leave me alone!" I shouted.

Loaf slapped me across the face. My cheek burned with pain and tears of mortification ran down my cheeks.

"Your dead capitalist parents can't help you now."

"Leave my parents out of it," I said, earning another stinging blow.

It took them fourteen days to break me: two weeks of labouring ten hours a day, tilling corners of the paddy missed by the ploughs, two weeks of struggle meetings, two weeks of night-long interrogation sessions in which Loaf's angry shouts blended with Zhao's soft inducements. Two weeks without rest. I was not allowed to wash or change my clothes. My body stank; my hair was matted with mud; my pant legs rotted off from the alkaline water that soaked into them in the paddies. Sometimes I was so disoriented I didn't know which room I was in, or what time it was.

When I was older I learned that I had been subjected to the kind of sleep-deprivation torture used by many countries in espionage and war. It was frequently practised by interrogators during the Cultural Revolution.

Finally, one night, Zhao spoke again. "Wouldn't you like to sleep, Xiao Ye? Wouldn't you like this to be over?"

"Tell me what you want me to write," I said, "and I'll do it."

To my everlasting shame, I filled two pages with untruths and exaggerations. I wrote that Representative Huang had criticized Cui and Zhao, which was true. I said that my friends and I had held meetings and criticized the PLA, which was false. My pages were sent back and forth to Cui and Zhao that night. They crossed things out, wrote comments in the margin, and I would rewrite the confession according to their "suggestions." Then, when it seemed I would finally be able to lie down, Cui insisted that I report everything that Yu Hua's sister, who was in the air force, had said to her about life in the military. Yu Hua had told me her sister frequently complained about the poor quality of the newly enlisted men and women and said that Lin Biao's son was a womanizer. At dawn they ordered me to sign the papers.

Even today I have never forgiven myself for informing on the only four people on the farm who treated me as a friend. We were singled out so that Cui and Zhao could prove that they had found and rooted out a counterrevolutionary conspiracy in their midst. Why had they chosen us over others? I had no way of knowing what I learned later—that my visit with Yu Hua to the sub-farm provided a means for Cui and Zhao, who were in the air force loyal to Lin Biao, to undermine the Shanghai Garrison by finding fault with Representative Huang.

After my confession was signed, my friends were released. But we were kept apart. Cui and Zhao told me they had sent their recommendation for punishment to higher authorities. We would certainly go to prison, they said. A real prison, not a labour camp. Only the length of the sentence remained to be decided.

—

I was no longer shadowed by Loaf or anyone else; however, every morning I was forced to bow my head before a life-sized statue of Chairman Mao set up in the middle of the compound at the crossroads. Although I kept telling myself not to take it too hard, I was always in tears when I finished. Until my house arrest and interrogation I had regarded myself as an old hand at dealing with humiliation, after the years of wearing my brothers' cast-off clothes and Number 2's unfitted glasses, after the begging trips with Mother, after living on welfare and enduring the insults of Red Guards. But nothing matched the inhuman treatment by Cui, Zhao and those they corrupted to do their work.

One very hot night in July, several days after my eighteenth birthday, I passed hour after hour of sleeplessness and depression. Finally, I pushed aside the mosquito netting, rose quietly from my bed and stole out of the dorm. I crept through the humid darkness as if in a trance, and reached the Sanlong River. I scrambled down the bank and waded in.

The river was deep, its surface like an ink stone, smooth and black. Between my toes, the cool bottom mud squashed, and the strong current tugged at my knees. I stood, taking in the silence and the heavy odour of water and earth from the paddies.

I only need to push off into the current, I thought, immerse my head, and suck the water deep into my lungs. It would be over quickly. I waded deeper.

I was up to my waist when I heard disembodied voices floating toward me. The hot night must have driven others out into the open air. As I prepared to take the plunge, a memory came to me. Several years before I had seen a drowned body pulled from Suzhou Creek near my home, so bloated that the shirt had split up the back and the trouser legs had parted at the seams.

I imagined my corpse lying like a piece of driftwood on the riverbank, limbs puffed like sausages, my face doughy. Strangers would manhandle my ugly, deformed body and throw me into a wagon for disposal.

I turned and fought the current to the riverbank, convinced that life was a prison, and that even death offered no escape.

If at the beginning of my interrogation the prisoners had been mean and cruel to me, some of them now tried to make things right. They looked at me with sympathy. Whenever I was washing or doing laundry, the stooped, white-haired old uncle who worked at the pump house would give me a rubber hose connected directly to the pump so that I didn't have to fetch water from the jars. I thanked him each time, but never learned his name. When I was too late to get my vacuum bottle filled with boiled water at the supply hut, a prisoner would take it over and have it filled in their hut. He always refused my penny. "You are one of us now," he would say. Though I appreciated his kindness, I often cried to think that I was on the same level as a criminal.

The busy rice-planting season was over and still no word came down about my jail sentence. No one seemed to care too much. Some students were friendly enough, but distant. I hadn't talked to Yu Hua since we had been arrested, not even when we bumped into one another. We were forbidden to speak to one another, but we could have got around that if we had wanted to. But things had changed between us. Our friendship had become a casualty of the purge. I wanted more than anything to tell her what I had done and to ask her forgiveness.

So I became even more withdrawn. When I was not working in the paddies, I kept to my bed, isolated under my mosquito netting. In early August, just when our workload lessened somewhat and I could breathe a little easier, I came down with malaria, a disease as common as colds in winter, but much more severe. Jia-ying added her blanket to mine, but the chill crept into my bones and I lay curled up in a ball until the tide of the disease turned and sweat soaked my clothes. In the breaks between attacks I lay feeble and exhausted, waiting for another onslaught. So many of us fell ill that a medical team was sent to the farm from Shanghai before the malaria got out of hand, and we were all urged to kill every mosquito under our nets before going to sleep.

The summer dragged on. In the fall, Cui and Zhao called a meeting to announce the sentences meted out to us "counter-revolutionary conspirators." We got two years each. We should consider ourselves lucky, Cui said, because he and Zhao had recommended five years. The sentencing was "semi-final," awaiting approval by the Shanghai Labour Reform Bureau, then under the Number Four Air Force Command.

That same night, while I was writing home to tell Great-Aunt and Number 2 the news that their Ah Si was going to jail, the girls in the dorm were all chattering about a greater tragedy. Xiao Jian, one of the three young men also sentenced, was the son of a man who had participated in the legendary Long March. When he learned that his son had been branded a counterrevolutionary, he told everyone in the family to cut off all relations with him. It was Xiao Jian who had "blinded his left eye," he claimed, referring to an injury he had sustained in the March. In her grief and shame, Xiao Jian's mother hanged herself in a closet.

Soon after, I learned how my "crimes" had affected my family. Number 2 had spent two years trying to join the

Communist Party. He was grateful to the Party because of their help during the factional battles among the workers in Shanghai, when he had barely escaped hanging. His application had been at long last accepted; finally, he thought, he would get away from the shadow of our bad class background. But when it was discovered that he had a counterrevolutionary sister, his bubble of hope burst. The Party rejected him. He was furious with me, and said so in his letter.

"I warned you to stay out of trouble," he wrote. "Obviously you didn't listen, and I must pay for your errors." If my own brother and adviser could blame me in that way, believing my accusers instead of me, what would my "revolutionary" Great-Aunt say? I felt abandoned by my own family.

My *tan-qin* was cancelled that February because I was still awaiting final word on my sentence. "It's a pity Representative Huang can't help you this time," Cui sneered as I left his office.

I dreaded the idea of going to prison, and kept the news away from Number 1 and Number 5. Until my arrival at the farm, I had never seen a real convict. In my childhood I had pictured criminals as green-faced, long-toothed monsters. How could I tell my eldest brother and my baby sister, who had their own problems, that I would soon be behind bars?

CHAPTER TWENTY

—

That spring I was strangely at peace. To people like Loaf, Leggy and Fatty I was now a non-person and they left me alone. To others I was invisible. To many more I was an example, a reminder of the rule, "Obey or be destroyed."

A whisper began to circulate around the farm. Three female students from our brigade, well-groomed and well-dressed, were swept away in a military jeep. Pretending to recruit talented young women for song and dance troupes, the air force was rounding up attractive young women to be mistresses for Lin Li-guo, Lin Biao's only son. Like an emperor and, as I learned many years later, like Mao himself, Lin Li-guo liked to surround himself with young virgins—who didn't remain virgins for long.

It was like a beauty contest. The candidates from each brigade were selected by the PLA reps, after their political backgrounds had been investigated. Political purity was the first criterion; next came beauty. The three women from our brigade returned the next afternoon, downcast. They had been turned down, and would have to stay on the farm.

That evening, as soon as political study had been concluded, the women in my dorm swirled around one of them, Xiao Hong, like a flock of sparrows. Where had the soldiers taken her? What had happened? Had she actually seen Lin Li-guo?

There had been a panel of seven judges to examine her. "All in uniform," she said. "They told me I was too big and tall, and that my feet were too long and wide! How can they expect us to have small feet when they know we work barefoot in the paddies for over six months a year?" she whined. "Why do they prefer small feet, anyway? Isn't that a feudal idea that was condemned a long time ago? Look at the women in the posters everywhere. Aren't they all big and strong?"

Xiao Hong went on to confirm the rumour that the recruitment had nothing to do with singing and dancing. "How could our leaders be lining up mistresses?" the women around her whispered. "How could the glorious PLA allow itself to be used in this manner?"

I overheard this conversation as I lay in bed. At one time I too would have been shocked to learn that the PLA would involve itself in such seamy practices, but Cui and Zhao had taught me otherwise. But China's leaders? That was a blow to what little idealism I had left. If the leaders were so corrupt, so hypocritical, how could anyone be safe?

"Do you know something, Xiao Ye?" Jia-ying confided from the bed beside mine. "If you were from a 'red' background, you would be a perfect candidate."

"Don't be silly!" I shot back, though I was half flattered.

I wondered how many of the women at the prison farm would have jumped at the chance to escape the farm and return to civilization, wear elegant and costly clothing, eat rich and carefully prepared food, enjoy sumptuous surroundings and, most important, live without politically motivated harassment.

"If you ever had the chance, would you go?" Jia-ying pressed.

Although I was eighteen, I knew nothing about intimate relations between men and women. Like many women my age, I was ignorant about sexual intercourse, or how babies were conceived or born. I was aware that to be Lin Li-guo's mistress was dissolute, but had no idea what such a role entailed.

"Well, would you?"

There were, as I knew now, only three ways to escape a lifetime of exile in this desolate and strife-ridden place: suicide, prison or selection as a mistress. I had tried the first. The second loomed over me.

"Yes," I whispered.

"So would I," said Jia-ying.

—

Since her return from her home visit the previous February, Jia-ying had changed. She was bolder now—the only one who would speak to me directly—and nothing seemed to intimidate her, not even Cui and Zhao. I surmised that something was in the air when she was transferred to the vegetable-growing team, an assignment we all considered heavenly. Usually only the PLA reps' favourites were given this privilege.

A couple of months later Jia-ying's mother showed up at the farm, shocking everyone, since parental visits were unheard of. She soon let it be known that her younger sister, Jia-ying's aunt, was married to Li Zheng-dao, a Chinese-American scientist who had won the 1957 Nobel Prize in Physics along with another Chinese-American, Yang Chen-ning. During the early phase of the Cultural Revolution, this "foreign connection" had worked against Jia-ying's family, causing them untold misery; but now that China–U.S. relations were improving, the family fortunes had been reversed and they had returned to the home from which they had been evicted several years before.

The same government that had encouraged Red Guards to pillage, beat and kill families like Jia-ying's was now "looking forward and forgetting the past" because of the change in relations with the United States. Although she was my friend and I was happy for her, I envied her unexpected good luck.

A week or so later word came that a woman from our sub-farm had been chosen by the panel selecting young virgins for Lin Li-guo. After a big farewell meeting she was paraded in a jeep from one village to another, waving to the crowds like a queen, then sent to the city of Guangzhou, where the young Lin lived.

"I told you so," Jia-ying said to me as we watched the procession. "Only in the Tang dynasty were big and tall women considered beautiful. That's why they turned down Xiao Hong."

I wished I had brought Number 2's glasses with me so that I could see what the fuss was about. All I could make out was a petite young woman in a blue Mao jacket, squeezed between two officers in the back seat of a jeep. In a society where beauty was officially labelled bourgeois, where femininity was condemned and where women and girls wore blue, brown or gray Mao suits, cut their hair short (unless they were young) and tried hard to look revolutionary, many women did not carry mirrors. I used the window glass to braid my pigtails.

Great-Aunt had once said, "A human being needs fine clothes the way a Buddha statue needs gold paint to enhance its glory." But I had grown up wearing my brothers' shabby clothes. How could I be good-looking, as Jia-ying had told me? No one else had ever even hinted that I was attractive. Until my friend made that remark I had never really thought much about how I looked to others, especially boys.

That evening I borrowed Jia-ying's mirror. Outside, in the fading light, careful not to be observed, I had a long look at myself. I saw a young woman with jet-black braids, an oval face with even teeth and large eyes with folded lids. Folded eyelids were considered more beautiful than unfolded.

The woman who looked back at me from the little mirror was not beautiful, I thought. Pleasant-looking, perhaps, and certainly not ugly, like Fatty or Loaf. But not lovely.

I recalled my first trip to the farm on the bus. Because I knew no one and I had sat alone on a seat for two, the boys had vied with each other to fall "accidentally" into the seat beside me. Absorbed in my feelings about leaving my family, I had paid no attention at the time, but now I wondered if they too had found me attractive. Was that why they had shyly offered me candy and cookies? Even after some people in my brigade had started to call me "Mila" after a pretty woman in an Albanian movie, I never took it seriously. But at least I didn't have a thick rump and ugly big breasts like Mila. Chinese standards of beauty preferred a small bosom and a flat bottom.

I turned the mirror over. What did it matter anyway? A woman with my bad blood could be as beautiful as a goddess and no one would give her the time of day.

—

By the time I walked into the summer of my nineteenth year, Lin Li-guo's vice had spread as far as the PLA reps.

Lao Chang had warned us when we first arrived at the farm that dating was prohibited; under Cui and Zhao any kind of relationship, even friendship, was persecuted. Men and women were prohibited from visiting one another in their dorms. When the hot weather drove us outdoors at night, the reps would lead search parties under the bridge piers and through the bushes, looking for couples—as if an innocent romance was a political crime. Those they found were humiliated and criticized at a meeting called for that purpose.

At one special criticism meeting, Cui read out a personal letter from a woman in my dorm, Zhen Bao, to her boyfriend, Wang Hua-shan, whose brother was married to Zhen's sister. Someone had stolen the letter from Wang and turned it in to

Cui, who read Zhen Bao's words out loud in a girlish voice, leering and mimicking, drawing sneers and laughter from some of the crowd. "'Thank god my period came yesterday,'" he read. The women near me gasped and shied away from this embarrassing declaration, but soon all of us, as expected and required, were shouting in unison, "Down with the hooligan Wang Hua-shan!" The next day, Wang was transferred to another sub-farm.

A few weeks later we were called together again and, on the way into the warehouse, forced to walk in single file past a table on which a dish and a Do Not Touch sign sat side by side. In the dish I saw a small shapeless object like a collapsed balloon. Next to the table, Yang, the tallest man in the village, stood with his head bowed. At the meeting, Zhao called Yang a dirty bastard for possessing a condom. Yang's girlfriend was criticized and ridiculed. The next day she tried to kill herself.

All this moral rectitude on the part of Cui and Zhao was pretense. We often saw them through the open windows and doors of the brick house, lying on their backs while girls, using two aluminum penny coins, plucked the hairs from their chins. Both reps openly petted and fondled willing female students. On more than one occasion a woman was sent packing. We learned later that these women had regained their city *hukou* as a "reward" for having an abortion and keeping their mouths shut.

Meanwhile I was still living in suspense, wondering when my jail sentence would be finalized and where I would serve it. There was no prison on the farm. Would they ship me off to a distant city? Then one day the five of us counterrevolutionary plotters were hauled up before the reps. It was a hot, humid July day, and the oscillating fan on Cui's desk clattered in vain. Yu, Zhu, Qian, Jian and I stood with our heads bowed as Zhao read sententiously from the paper in his hand.

"For forming a counterrevolutionary clique and attempting to undermine the PLA, your sentence of two years is confirmed."

My heart sank. In spite of myself I had been hoping that someone above Cui and Zhao would have some common sense, or take pity on me and my friends. But it was not to be. I steeled myself for what came next, certain that I would be sent even farther from home.

Zhao cleared his throat. "Sentence to be served supervised by the masses."

I could hardly believe my ears. I clamped my lips shut to hold back any expression of relief and fought to keep myself from glancing at my friends. It was an anticlimax, after all. I would not be shipped off to a prison. The charge and sentence would be recorded in my dossier. I would lose my *tan-qin* for the duration of my sentence. But "supervised by the masses" meant that I would continue as I had been since my release from interrogation—working as normal under the nominal scrutiny of everyone. The reps' recommendation for our imprisonment had been repudiated at a higher level.

My four friends were split up and sent away to different brigades. I was not even allowed to say goodbye to them. If not for Jia-ying, I would have felt completely alone.

CHAPTER TWENTY-ONE

—

Cui often said that it was better to "reap proletarian weeds than sow capitalist seeds." That autumn he got what he wanted. The rice harvest was so meagre that Lao Chang said it would have cost the government less money to have us sit around and do nothing, for the yield hardly repaid the investment of seed, equipment and fertilizer, let alone our wages and months of labour.

But for me, the poor harvest was more than balanced by good news. September 24, 1971 was a typically crisp fall day, a welcome relief after the long season of heat and humidity. When I awoke that morning I heard someone shouting outside.

I rushed out of the dorm, rubbing the sleep from my eyes. A young man stood in front of the reps' brick house, hands cupped around his mouth, yelling, "They're gone! They're gone!"

People began to run toward him. I hung back, afraid of a trick. But after everyone converged on the house, I joined them. The structure was empty, stripped bare of furniture, posters, even the photo of Mao and Lin Biao. "Where have they gone?" everyone asked, but no one knew. Many made guesses. I kept my mouth firmly closed.

The speculation and gossip continued for a week, until one day, as we made our way to the fields, Representative Huang of the Shanghai Garrison pulled up in a jeep with an officer I had never seen. Huang directed everyone except the prisoners to go to the warehouse immediately for an important meeting. When we were all assembled he wasted no time on formalities.

"The traitor Lin Biao, his wife and son are dead. The plane they had commandeered for their escape to the Soviet Union crashed in Outer Mongolia."

No one spoke. We were stunned. Vice Chairman Lin Biao a traitor? Once again someone we had been taught to revere was now being called a stinking heap of animal dung. More than three weeks before, Huang told the silent assembly, Lin had fled when his plot to assassinate Mao and take over the government by military coup was uncovered.

Huang went on to admonish us not to speak of these events. An official investigation conducted by Premier Zhou En-lai himself was under way, and since our farm had been under the authority of Lin Biao and had figured largely in his plans as a base, some people's lives were at stake. When he spoke these words, many turned their eyes toward me. I stared straight ahead, numb with fear.

No wonder Cui and Zhao had run off. They were associated with the PLA faction loyal to Lin Biao. Now the work to make the road fit for military vehicles made sense. Lin Biao had been preparing for possible civil war.

And so the tables were turned yet again. Another movement began, a rectification campaign criticizing Lin Biao and all those in his camp. What had been white was now black. Our nights were filled with political study, reading and discussing documents denouncing Lin Biao and his counterrevolutionary activities. Now, all the evil stupidities of the Cultural Revolution carried out on our farm—from the neglect of the fields to friends informing on each other—were blamed on Lin Biao and our departed PLA reps. Even Leggy bragged that she had harboured doubts about the reps as she took part in the merciless interrogation of me and my friends. I seethed at the hypocrisy. It wasn't Lin Biao but the people around me who had persecuted me.

In the end, my four friends and I were brought together for a rehabilitation meeting at the sub-farm. What had been black was now white. Gatherings like this were supposed to cancel all the harm that had been done. Our malicious treatment was blamed on the dead. But exoneration tasted like ashes in my mouth. Was I expected to be grateful that we were not counterrevolutionaries after all? Our innocence, friendship and trust had been shattered. None of us talked about what had happened or what we had said and written under torture. None of us discussed our detention. More than ever I wanted to tell Yu Hua, Xiao Jian, Xiao Qian and Xiao Zhu what I had said and done, to clear the air. I craved their forgiveness, even though I could hardly remember the things I had "admitted."

On my visit home that winter, after a two-year absence, Number 2 bought me a new short-wave radio and a set of recently published English textbooks. The gifts were his way of showing his concern for my suffering and apologizing for the letter in which he had criticized me for ruining his chances to join the Party.

"Shanghai Radio Station has started broadcasting English lessons as a positive signal to the United States," he said. "You always liked English, Ah Si, so maybe you can continue learning it."

Holding the books in my hand, I could not speak, for my throat was thick with emotion. I was touched by his generosity. I knew he was still paying off the loans he had taken out to help Number 5 and me prepare to go to the countryside.

But I was also filled with sadness because I could not bring myself to tell him the details of my ordeal or what I had done to my friends. Nor would Great-Aunt be a help. Even she was saying how she had always had a bad feeling about Lin Biao's "conspiratorial looks."

"He had ghostlike features," she claimed, "with those tiny triangle eyes under bushy brows. That pale smiling face always gave me goose bumps." Hindsight can be blinding.

—

Two months after I returned to the farm, news came that there was a shortage of manpower in Shanghai, from sales-clerks to street-sweepers, from prison guards to teachers. The chaos of the Cultural Revolution had killed many by suicide, execution, beatings or battles, and hundreds of thousands had been sent to the countryside. A number of us would be chosen to return to the city to fill some of the jobs, and the farm buzzed with excitement and speculation as everyone tried in vain to keep their hopes in check. Hope, we all knew to our cost, was mother to disappointment. People around me thought I might have a chance to become a teacher because, ironically, a pure class background was not necessary for that role. To avoid frustration, I fought hard to remain unenthusiastic about my chances. It won't happen, I kept telling myself. Yu Hua was selected to be a prison guard. When Jian, Qian and Zhu were assigned teaching posts I began to hope in spite of myself. Delirious with joy, they packed up and left the farm for good.

But all four of them were "red" students and I was not. Our new rep, Meng, said that I must remain on the farm. He explained that I needed more hardship to overcome my "bourgeois weakness."

There were more changes. A newly formed civilian leadership took control of the farm, replacing PLA reps and self-appointed students' committees. We moved across the bridge into houses with brick walls and thatched roofs—a great improvement over the damp wattle buildings in which I had spent the last four years.

I passed what little free time we were allowed on my bed, listening to my new radio and studying English. Although I was hurt and extremely bitter, as well as lonely, I reached a separate peace. My roommates pitied me and left me alone or jeered at me for "drawing water with a bamboo basket"—wasting my time studying a useless language. They could not understand that I wanted to be by myself and stay out of trouble. Nor did they know how much I thirsted for love and friendship.

And yet sometimes I thought of myself as a cold and insensitive creature not fit for this world. After all the persecution, insults, lies and betrayals, I didn't know how to deal with matters of the heart like love and trust.

—

On my home visit the following winter I met Number 5 at the train station. Both of us were at a low point of our lives: trapped on our respective farms, watching in helpless frustration as our farm-mates left for city jobs and gained a city *hu-kou* through connections or "earned" it through good political background. Nevertheless, we agreed that we would try to make our two-week visit a cheerful event, especially since Number 1 was to be married. It was to be our first gathering as a family since I had been sent into exile four years before.

Number 1's marriage was the fruit of matchmaking and the postal service. I was sad to see my eldest brother give up his belief in love. I remembered, during his first year at university, his conversation with Mother when he found out she had been secretly arranging a marriage for him. Number 1 had told her that times had changed, that the government encouraged the abandonment of feudal customs like arranged marriages. He would choose his own wife, he vowed, and marry her for love.

But in the meantime Number 1, a deeply intelligent man with a once-promising future, had been stripped of his Shanghai *hu-kou* and sent to a remote and backward mountainous area in Guizhou Province to work in a tool repair shop. There he had been confronted with reality. If he married a local woman, he would have to spend the rest of his life there, and so would his children. He would not see us again because the home-visit policy would no longer apply. So he agreed to exchange letters and photos with a young woman named Yu-qin, who lived in Shanghai. The whole arrangement was a gamble. No one knew when the young couple would be able to live together, if ever. But marrying a Shanghai resident was Number 1's only hope.

In China it is the groom's responsibility to pay for and host the wedding. The ceremony was held at home, with the two families having dinner together. I couldn't remember the last time there had been so much food on our table in Purple Sunshine Lane. There was chicken stewed in soup, duck simmered in soybean sauce, steamed fish and braised pig's legs, along with stir-fried vegetables—much of it bought by Number 3 in the Songjiang black market. The duck and chicken must be cooked and served whole, Great-Aunt had insisted, to symbolize the unity of the new family. It was a happy moment, but my heart was heavy with sorrow and contradiction. Number 1 had given up his dream and, like most people, married for practical reasons. What advantage was there for Yu-qin, his new wife? I wondered. She seemed pleasant enough, but was also loud and brash.

It seemed that history was repeating itself. Father and Mother had lived apart for a long time after their marriage. Looking at my smiling brother, I was overwhelmed with sadness. I found Great-Aunt in the kitchen and told her I was going for a walk to get some fresh air. My face must have signalled my thought, for she didn't argue. It was dark and cold outside and the streets were almost deserted. Probably everyone was feasting, I thought, the main activity of the New Year celebrations. With nowhere to go, no friends to visit, I wandered the streets for hours.

A couple of months later Number 1 wrote to me with good and bad news. Yu-qin was pregnant, but she had been listed as one of those to be sent to work in a small town in Anhui Province, northwest of Shanghai, another undeveloped area of the country.

As with so many people in those days, Fate had played a trick on my new sister-in-law. Both Yu-qin's parents were workers. When she had graduated from junior middle school, she had chosen to enroll in a trade school attached to a factory. Such a choice was a last resort, made by those who couldn't get into a normal middle school, and involved a major loss of face for both the student and the family. But subsequently the humiliation was paid back when Yu-qin saw her contemporaries who had made it into good schools sent to the countryside, while she, a worker, and therefore exalted, remained in Shanghai.

But the blessing was short-lived. Now married and pregnant, and with her husband in faraway Guizhou, she was transferred. She was able to postpone her departure until her baby was born, then she left for Anhui, taking her son, Ye Xiang, with her. Ten months later, after he had been weaned, she brought him back to Shanghai and left him in Great-Aunt's care. Number 1 still had not seen his son.

And so Great-Aunt, at sixty-three, suffering from high blood pressure, began to care for the fourth generation of the Ye family, who had taken her in and given her a place to live more than forty years before. But now the Ye family was scattered, and she cared for the baby alone.

CHAPTER TWENTY-TWO

—

In March 1973, Deng Xiao-ping was brought back to power as vice-premier of China, after years of disgrace. Within a month the "Suggestions for University Enrollment" was issued by the Party's Central Committee. Deng realized the need for educated people after years of turmoil throughout the school system. Until then, a person who had worked in a unit for at least two years and had a recommendation from his or her unit leaders and co-workers could get into university without taking entrance exams. These were the "Worker-Peasant-Soldier" students. Deng's declaration stated that Worker-Peasant-Soldier candidates must sit for exams, although their scores would not be the sole criteria; for university entrance political correctness would also count.

I took this as a sign that things might be returning to normal and was encouraged in my English study, though I dared not hope that I would ever get a chance at university. Just a couple of weeks before, my application to be a taxi driver in Shanghai had been refused. The farm's new civilian leader, Sun, told me that as the youngest of the experienced hands in the brigade I should let the older men and women go back to the city first. Instead I was assigned as "elder sister" to a batch of newly arrived seventeen-year-old girls, to show them the ropes. For days and nights I was like a firefighter, running out one door and in another, except that I put out tears instead of flames. My heart went out to the miserable teenagers. They were about the same age as I had been when I first came to the farm and they were depressed, scared and homesick. I did the best I could to teach them everything, from the differences between rice seedlings and grass to the best way to hang their laundry to avoid insect contamination. I was an old hand now, I realized without joy, a veteran with calluses on my palms and on the soles of my feet—and, I sometimes thought, on my soul. But using my five years of experience to help them gave me great satisfaction.

—

In May of the following year I learned that our farm had been allotted ten slots for university enrollment. One of them was for an English major.

My heart leapt. Was this my chance? Or was it nonsense to even consider that I would get the support of the brigade to take the exam, even though I had been studying English alone for two years? The summer before, I had applied to go to Fudan University to study Spanish, but the unit had turned me down, once again citing seniority.

But this seemed to be a more auspicious time. I had now been on the farm for almost six years and, according to the regulations, if I was successful I could take my salary with me to university. I would not need to ask my family for support. I filled out the application.

The votes of the young women to whom I had acted as an elder sister tipped the count in my direction. My unexpected success at getting over this first hurdle gave me sleepless nights. The next obstacle was another selection: the farm was made up of thirty brigades, and each had elected a candidate. Now the administration would select fifteen from the thirty to take the medical exam. Those who passed it would sit the entrance exam.

I was encouraged that Representative Huang, who had quashed my attempt to return to Shanghai as a teacher—probably because he found out I had written something about him in my confession—had nothing to do with the present selection process.

So I waited, trying not to think about it as I laboured, bent double, in the paddies. One afternoon, as I washed the mud from my legs and feet, I heard that the medical team had arrived at the sub-farm. I entered the dorm and sat on my bed, afraid to move, and asked someone to bring back my supper from the canteen: I didn't want to be away from my dorm in case I was sent for. Hours passed by and no one came. The village got darker and quieter, and my heartbeat soared each time I heard approaching footsteps. But there was no news.

I woke up in the morning fully clothed, with a severe headache. I had failed again. I tried to put it out of my mind, but it was hard. I dragged myself out of bed and to the canteen.

I was lugging bundles of seedlings on my shoulder-pole, heading to the paddy, when I was hailed by a man out of breath from running.

"Xiao Ye, someone has telephoned from the sub-farm," he blurted, stopping to gulp down some air. "They're asking why you didn't show up for your medical checkup. The doctors are about to leave and—"

I threw down my shoulder-pole, scattering the green seedlings on the dike, and ran toward the paddy where brigade leader Sun was working. As soon as he caught sight of me he shrieked.

"*Ai yah!* I forgot to tell you—"

"How could you forget such a thing? How could you!" I cried.

Sun and I rushed back to his office, where he snatched up the phone and frantically wound the handle. He spoke to the operator and asked her to tell the doctors to wait.

"We're on our way," he said, hanging up. "Come on, Xiao Ye, we'll take my bike!"

After bumping along the dirt roads, sidesaddle on the rat-trap carrier of Sun's bike, I found myself in the clinic, feet, legs and hands still caked with paddy mud, talking to a group of white-clothed doctors. They did their best to calm me down, then conducted the examination.

The next day I was to have a blood test for hepatitis. This was another hurdle. Hepatitis was widespread throughout the country and our farm was no exception. The number of cases had climbed in the past few years because of contaminated water and poor and crowded living conditions. When I got up early the next morning, having eaten or drunk nothing overnight as ordered, I was showered with advice.

"My mother said sugar makes the liver softer," said Xiao Jiang, one of the newer girls. "That's why hepatitis patients get extra sugar coupons."

I drank the proffered cup of sugar-water and immediately felt guilty for cheating. Later, as the doctor drew my blood, I confessed.

"Don't worry," he said. "I have two daughters and one of them is your age. She is working on a farm in Heilongjiang Province. I hope someday she will get a chance like yours." He didn't tell me, though, whether the sugar-water would help me or not. My health was pronounced excellent.

So, more waiting. I was anxious about the coming exam. I felt confident I could pass, given all my studying of textbooks and the English lessons on the radio; but nothing was ever simple or clear.

One afternoon in August I was called from the paddies once more and told to go to the sub-farm administration office. This time I remembered to wash off the mud in a ditch. Xiao Zhao, a young man who worked in the canteen, took me on his bike. All I had with me was a ball-point pen.

The sub-farm was quiet, a usual weekday afternoon, with everyone in the paddies. I hopped down from the bike, thanked Xiao Zhao, and went to the office. There I was directed to a room down the hall. I remembered the day of my middle-school entrance exams. There were flags snapping in the breeze outside the buildings, hundreds of students and their families milling around on the sidewalks, row upon row of desks in the sultry classroom. Mother had been alive then, and the most important issue challenging my young mind had been which middle school I would go to. Now, at twenty-two, I faced the most important test of my life. Success meant a brighter future. Failure would bring more of the same misery.

I stepped into the small room, where two middle-aged women, with their hair cut plainly at earlobe length, sat behind desks, fanning themselves. It was hot and stuffy. An armchair sat forlornly in a corner; a single desk and chair had been placed before the two women; the bamboo window curtains were drawn against the afternoon sun. I looked around, wondering where the other candidates were. The examiners rose.

"There is no one else here," said one, who looked to be in her fifties. She smiled. "Yours is the only exam."

In my nervousness I completely missed the significance of her words.

"I am Teacher Chen from Beijing University," she went on. "Teacher Xu is from Qinghua University."

I nodded at the younger, stern-looking woman.

"We are recruiting students from East China," Teacher Chen explained.

My brain began to function. "Do you mean that you came down here just for one candidate?"

"This by no means suggests that you will be successful," Teacher Xu cut in, indicating that I should sit down. "Now, let's begin."

She handed me a piece of paper on which a few passages in classical Chinese were printed. "Please translate them into everyday speech."

I took out my pen and began. It was not difficult; my first semester in middle school had been devoted to this kind of work. About an hour later, I put down my pen. My second test was oral. Teacher Chen gave me a text in English called "We Have Friends All Over the World" and asked me to read it out loud. I didn't need to translate, just read. It was a piece I had read over many times at night under my mosquito net, for it was in one of the books Number 2 had given me.

Now all my studying in isolation, while my dorm-mates played cards, chatted or crocheted, paid off. I read out the text, clear and loud. Teacher Chen could barely contain her pleasure. Teacher Xu maintained her serious demeanour and reminded me that, although I had done well, that didn't mean I would be selected.

"One red heart, two preparations," she admonished me—a good person should be prepared for failure as well as success—a common expression around exam time at school.

I stood up and forced myself to look her straight in the eye. "Please," I stammered, "please let me go to university. I have been here for six years, working in the paddies the whole time.

Don't you think I have got enough education from the peasants, as Chairman Mao wishes? I promise you, if you accept me, I'll never let you down."

When I turned around and left the room, Teacher Chen followed me. As we shook hands, she looked into my eyes and squeezed my hand.

On the way back to the village I was deep in thought. I had done my best and said what I wanted to say to the two teachers. Now I would have to let Fate take care of the rest. And yet, why was there only one person to take the exam? And what was Teacher Chen trying to tell me when she squeezed my hand?

CHAPTER TWENTY-THREE

—

By that time I had been "dating" Xiao Zhao, the young man in the canteen, for a few months—the old prohibitions had been relaxed. It was the first relationship for both of us, although he was much sought after by the pretty women in our village. Nicknamed Huang-di—King—for his good looks, Xiao Zhao was three years older than me, the seventh of eight children in his family. His mother had died of a heart attack when he was seven and his father had remarried.

Like mine, his parents had been Shanghai business people. Though we came from the same background and had arrived at the farm on the same day, we had walked different paths. While the majority struggled in the paddies, buffeted by the northwest wind, he had worked in the canteen from the beginning—one of the plum jobs in the village. Xiao

Zhao hadn't suffered persecution like the rest of us with tainted blood. In fact, under Representatives Zhao and Cui he had been designated a "Five Goods" Worker—outstanding in five stated areas of political correctness—every year.

My first contact with Xiao Zhao had come after I was released from house arrest. I had been summoned to the brick house and told by Cui to prepare for another struggle meeting that night. By the time he let me go, supper was over. I took my food tin to the canteen, entered the darkened dining room and knocked on one of the serving windows. Xiao Zhao opened the window, took my tin and returned a few moments later, having gone to the trouble of heating up the food for me. I was grateful for the kindness and thanked him.

"Do you really think what you are going through is worth the trouble?" he asked, handing me the food through the serving window. "Why not just go along with them? Take my advice, don't push against the wind."

I didn't speak to him again for two years, then a very strange thing happened. I was at home in Shanghai and my two-week *tan-qin* was drawing to an end. Number 3 found me in a nearby store where I was doing some last-minute shopping for my return.

"There is an old man in our apartment," she exclaimed, "and he has a big parcel with him. He says he wants you to take it back to the farm and give it to his son."

I was at a loss. No one at Da Feng had asked me for a favour.

"He's well dressed," Number 3 went on, "with a heavy Ningbo accent. Judging by the way he talks, I bet he used to be a boss."

I hurried home to find a man exactly as Number 3 had described. Showing me a piece of paper with my address on it, he said that his son, Xiao Zhao, had written and asked him to come and request the favour. He knew his son had said nothing to me.

On the day I arrived back at the farm, Xiao Zhao came to my dorm to pick up his package. He apologized for not asking me ahead of time for the favour. I was confused and too shy to ask him where he had acquired my address.

One day the following spring when I came back from the paddies for lunch, Xiao Zhao met me at my dorm.

"Do you have any fresh water?" he asked. "The pump is not working."

From then on, he would visit our dorm a couple of nights each week. Many of the girls were happy to see him. He would say "Hello, everyone!" and be entertained by hopeful females, plied with cookies and tea. But gradually he spent more and more time talking to me, and it soon became clear that I was the one he had come to visit.

For the first time, I had someone to talk to. Tentatively, Xiao Zhao asked me about my house arrest, but I gave him no details. I was still ashamed of myself and had decided to take my shame to the grave. Most people didn't want to relive those days. "Look to the future," they would say, "there's no use refrying old rice." Nevertheless, I was thankful for his concern.

Xiao Zhao was a kind and sympathetic listener, and our talks were the start of our relationship. I was flattered that he had chosen me when so many women were attracted to him, but at first I was reluctant to begin dating him, and said so.

"Is it because you haven't written back to your pal Xiao Qian yet?"

"How did you know about that?"

He laughed. "Oh, I have friends in the post office."

He kept our relationship from his family. He was worried that his parents, especially his father, would reject it. Boss Zhao, a strict traditional Chinese father whose authority extended to every aspect of his children's lives, especially their choice of partner, had insisted that Xiao Zhao not involve himself in any relationship until he left the farm. That was why Xiao Zhao had resisted all the women who would have loved to be his girlfriend.

"It was you I was interested in," he told me, "ever since I saw you the first time."

"Why did you wait so long to let me know?"

"Well," he answered, "you always seemed to be in trouble of one kind or another."

Although it was not the answer I wanted to hear, I accepted it. At least he was frank with me.

I didn't tell anyone in my family about him, either. I didn't know how long our relationship would last; most of those on the farm were short-lived. Besides, I didn't want another reason for Great-Aunt to get stirred up.

On the day I took my exam, Xiao Zhao came to see me in the evening. We sat outside the dorm, as usual. I was utterly exhausted, but peaceful. Xiao Zhao was unusually quiet. Finally he spoke.

"Tell me. Will you drop me like a sack of potatoes if you get into university?"

"Of course not!" I answered. "Why are you talking about this? You shouldn't. It's bad luck to talk about events in advance." Great-Aunt's superstitions had had an effect on me and I thought for a moment he was trying to put a curse on my chance by predicting success before the results were known. I hoped my quick response would make him drop the subject.

But he ignored me. "You are going to be a student at Bei Da"—the short form for Beijing University—"one of the best in China. And I probably will stay here for the rest of my life, being a peasant." He emphasized the last word, although strictly speaking he was not a peasant; he did not work in the fields.

"Just drop it," I said. "I don't want to talk about it any more. We can discuss it when the time comes."

"No," he insisted again. "It will be too late then. I want you to promise now, tonight. Will you abandon me or not?"

"You've got your answer." I got up and went inside the dorm.

I didn't sleep that night. With no preparation, suddenly Xiao Zhao had forced me to make a serious commitment. I had often heard the heartbroken sobbing of those who had been abandoned by their "city *hu-kou*" boyfriends and had joined in condemning their unfaithfulness. It became clear to me that I would have no option if I was accepted at Bei Da, at least if Xiao Zhao was still on the farm. Duty would now prohibit me from breaking off with him.

It was ten long days later that the news came. I was in my dorm after the day's work, fetching my food tin, when Sun knocked on the door and stepped inside.

"Xiao Ye. I just got a phone call."

My tin dropped from my hands, my throat went dry and my temples pounded. "What did they say?"

A smile broke across Sun's narrow face. "You've been accepted. Go to the sub-farm tomorrow and fill out the enrollment forms."

My hands began to shake. Soon my whole body was trembling and I had to sit down. I laid my head on the table and covered it with my arms. I was going to be a university student. Suddenly, unbelievably, a bright ray of sunshine lit up my future. I wished my parents could know, and, thinking of them, I began to weep quietly. Now Great-Aunt could be proud of me. Now the burden of guilt at my replacing her on the farm would lift itself from Number 3's shoulders. Now I could help my little sister.

"Congratulations, Xiao Ye," Sun said, pulling the door closed as he left.

The word spread quickly and I was showered with good wishes. I was the first ever in our brigade to go to university since we had arrived here six years before. The next morning, after a night without rest, I went to the sub-farm office. My hand shook as I filled out the enrollment paper with my name on it.

I learned that my acceptance notice had been sitting in a desk drawer since my exams took place, but no one had bothered to tell me.

It was difficult to grasp the fact that my days as a peasant labourer in the unyielding paddies were over. Except for Xiao Zhao and a few supportive friends, I had no one to say goodbye to. Certainly I would not miss the stark, unfriendly landscape or the northwest wind. I remembered poor Jia-ying. Soon after her transfer to the vegetable-growing team, her brother had come to visit her and the two of them spent the afternoon together in the dorm with no others around, causing some women to gossip behind her back and men to laugh at her in front of her face, accusing her of incest. The shame and humiliation drove her to mental instability and she was sent back to Shanghai. I remembered my four "counterrevolutionary" friends and the ordeal that shattered our unity; the days of unearned ostracism and disgrace; the struggle meetings; and always, the thousands of hours of backbreaking labour.

I had entered my twenty-third year. Up till now my existence had been controlled by fate, political storm, and loss. Maybe now I could lay my hand on the rudder of my own life and steer out of the bitter sea.

(Left) my ID photo for the prison farm where I laboured for six years (1968–74) and was persecuted as a "counterrevolutionary."
(Right) My Beijing University ID photo, autumn 1974.

CHAPTER TWENTY-FOUR

—

"Ah Si of the Ye family is going to Bei Da to learn to speak a foreign language." The news was running up and down Purple Sunshine Lane. Old neighbours came to the apartment to congratulate me and new ones marvelled at what a lucky creature I was. One old woman in the next building, whom everyone called "old chamber-pot cleaning lady," claimed that she had always known from the shape of my forehead that I had a bright future.

The only one not thrilled by the news was Great-Aunt. Having always believed that reading and writing were the business of men, she was unimpressed with the prospect of my being a university student. She was getting older and weaker, and all she wanted was for the daughter she had never had to be home again with her after six years.

Before I left, I went to the hospital to see Number 2. He had broken his leg in an accident at work and had suffered through three operations. Smiling weakly, he handed me a used copy of the Oxford English-Chinese Dictionary.

"I fished it out of a garbage pail years ago when the Red Guards were on a book-burning spree."

How typical of my brother, who loved learning, to put himself in danger over a dictionary.

Number 3 saw me off at the station. I hugged her for the first time in our lives.

"I am no longer on the farm, Ah Sei," I told her. "That means you are free now, too."

Weeping freely, Number 3 embraced me again.

When the train stopped at Wuxi station to discharge and take on passengers, I thought sadly about my parents. I hadn't been able to visit their grave on my way to Beijing; Auntie Yi-feng had written to me that since the Red Guards had toppled and broken the headstone, the peasants had carted away the pieces and used them for construction, then planted crops on the land, obscuring the grave site.

I wondered if my parents would be proud of me now, and vowed that some day I would return to the land of fish and rice to find their grave and raise a stone again in their memory.

AFTERWORD

—

After three and a half years at Beijing University studying English Language and Literature—and after still more political turmoil—I graduated and was recruited by the national government to work as an interpreter in Shanghai. I interpreted for official delegations from Africa, Europe, Thailand, Australia, Great Britain, the United States, and Canada, meeting, among others, kings, prime ministers, presidents, the First Lady of the United States, and Queen Elizabeth.

When I was thirty-five, I came to York University in Canada as a Visiting Scholar and decided to stay. I left the university and worked as a baby-sitter, office assistant and bank clerk. I published my first book in 1997.

As soon as I gained my Canadian citizenship and could travel back to China without fear of reprisal for my defection, I went to Qingyang and raised a new monument on my parents' grave.

I am now a full-time writer and return to Shanghai often to visit my family.

bourgeois: a critical term for not following Party policy and for being counterrevolutionary.

capitalist class: one of the social groups identified by the Communists, referring to those who used to be business owners before the Communists gained power in 1949. The term also applied to the family members of the business owners.

capitalist roaders: Party officials who fell out of Mao Ze-dong's favour and were accused of betraying Party policies and taking the path of capitalism.

class struggle: fights between various social groups identified by the government, mainly between the working class and the capitalist class.

da-zi-bao, xiao-zi-bao: posters, forms of political expression used by people to voice their support of Party policies or to attack political rivals.

Deng Xiao-ping: moved in and out of power at Mao's whim. He regained importance at the end of the Cultural Revolution, and became top man after 1977.

the Five Blacks: a category of politically "un-pure" people including former landlords, rich peasants, counterrevolutionaries, rightists, and former capitalists.

the Five Reds: a category of politically "pure" people including factory workers, poor and lower-middle-class peasants, soldiers and officers of the People's Liberation Army, Party officials, and those who died for the revolution.

the Four Olds: old culture, old customs, old habits and old ways of thinking, attacked during the Cultural Revolution because they would drag China back into the pre-revolutionary past.

Gang of Four: (*Si Ren Bang*) Jiang Qing, Wang Hong-wen, Zhang Chun-qiao, and Yao Wen-yuan. Before the Cultural Revolution, they were low-ranking officials. They used the Great Proletarian Cultural Revolution to gain power.

Great Proletarian Cultural Revolution (GPCR): a political movement launched by Mao Ze-dong in 1966 to renew the spirit of the Communist Revolution that established the People's Republic of China in 1949. Mao feared that China was slipping back into the old ways. The ten-year movement was primarily used to keep Mao and his supporters in power.

hu-kou: a booklet normally held by the head of a family which listed the name, birthday, gender, and political background of everyone who lived in the household, along with their relationships to one another. The *hu-kou* was also a person's official registration document for residence, either rural or urban. It was extremely difficult, almost impossible, to have a rural *hu-kou* changed to an urban one.

Jiang Qing: Mao Ze-dong's fourth wife and member of the Gang of Four.

9th Communist Party Congress (April, 1969) in Beijing: this was a big event. A congress was supposed to be held every year, but the 9th was the first since 1956. Here Mao Ze-dong and his supporters consolidated their power and firmly established the Cultural Revolution. Lin-Biao was named Mao Ze-dong's successor.

Lin Biao: a military leader who fought for China's revolution for 22 years. He held several positions of power in the government and communist party, and supported the Cultural Revolution. In 1971 he was accused of plotting to overthrow Mao Ze-dong. He died with his family in a plane crash while trying to escape from China.

Little Red Treasure Book: actually titled *Quotations from Chairman Mao*— excerpts from Mao Ze-dong's writings.

Liu Shao-qi: President of the People's Republic of China 1959–1966. During the Cultural Revolution he was branded Number One Capitalist Roader and thrown into prison where he died in 1969 after three years of physical abuse and mental torture.

PLA: the People's Liberation Army in reality included all military services—army, air force, navy.

purge: a political term describing the removal of one's opponents from their positions, usually by execution or imprisonment.